# The Worst Resume Ever Written

**Veronica Vulpine**

authorHOUSE®

*AuthorHouse™*
*1663 Liberty Drive*
*Bloomington, IN 47403*
*www.authorhouse.com*
*Phone: 1 (800) 839-8640*

*Published by AuthorHouse 10/26/2017*

*ISBN: 978-1-5462-1460-1 (sc)*
*ISBN: 978-1-5462-1459-5 (e)*

*Print information available on the last page.*

*Any people depicted in stock imagery provided by Thinkstock are models, and such images are being used for illustrative purposes only. Certain stock imagery © Thinkstock.*

*This book is printed on acid-free paper.*

*Because of the dynamic nature of the Internet, any web addresses or links contained in this book may have changed since publication and may no longer be valid. The views expressed in this work are solely those of the author and do not necessarily reflect the views of the publisher, and the publisher hereby disclaims any responsibility for them.*

Dedicated to Richard Bundy, Gregg Brilliant,
and Mike Chrysanthemum, the only people
to tell me that I should be a writer.

Also, Thank you, Robert Rambles,
for always believing in me!

Caution: This novella contains much
profanity and belligerence!

# Chapter 1

I once worked with a guy that I deemed Little Kevin. This was obviously because his name was Kevin, and he WAS little. I started telling him all the jobs that I have had, to which he seemed horrified. I guess when mommy and daddy paid for his engineering degree education he probably became a little judgmental.

# Chapter 2

<u>Sugarmans.</u> (Now, when I wrote this, I tried to change as many names of companies as I could, because I did not want to get sued, but the fact that both however both this place is now defunct, and I just couldn't morph the title with anything creative, I just really don't give a shit. Here is my list of possible ideas: Sugardaddies (which sounds like a place where trophy wives, or strippers come to meet their dream man), Sugarhands, (which either said hotties would either come for a manicure or be employed as masseuses), Sugarglands (which said attractive women would probably be performing strange sexual acts of prostrate stimulation), Sugarfans (which sounds like a childrens' novel involving fairies with incredibly quick wing momentum, Sugarbits (which sounds like a lot a breakfast cereal), or Sugarcans (which sounds like a recycling center). Oh, just screw it already!

Anyway, when I was 16, I was hired for this company to address all their advertising issues. This meant I would come in on 6:00 A.M. on a Sunday morning, check the ads in the papers for typos for prices, and then I would basically forge paperwork for the Funday Times to cease the costumers' incessant bitching. Please keep in mind that this was before Photoshop, so a lot of White-Out and cut and pasting at the Xerox machine was involved with fake letterheads. It was like the most shadiest arts and crafts show ever exhibited.

Sugarmans. This is actually almost terrifying. I am upstairs there at about 8:00 P.M. (Now keep in mind that this is before cell phones were invented.) All of these offices are dead empty, and I'm up there doing advertising. This was the horrible thing, whatever electrical genius did the wiring, only put one switch for the hallway lights at the FAR end were my computer office was. So this basically meant walking in pitch black down the hallway to turn on the lights, and on exiting, obviously, the complete opposite. Pitch black, once again, past all the empty offices.

One night I am up there working once again, by myself, and the big black phone rings. All I heard when I answered it was heavy breathing and a voice that said, "I know you're up there all alone, and I'm going to get you." CLICK! Now, I am very aware of the flight or fight syndrome, so when presented with unprecedented horror, I can honestly admit that I become completely unglued at any given such situation. Not having an outside line or the downstairs extension numbers or having anyone being able to hear me downstairs even if I blew out my vocal cords screaming, I believed I had only two options available. The first was to shut the composite door, basically constructed of cardboard with no lock on it, and try to barricade myself in with every piece of office equipment possible, praying the axe murderer would pretty much not have an axe. The second would be to kill all the lights and try to escape as stealthily as possible and pray the psycho was not hiding in one of the empty offices... with an AXE! I chose the latter option, and by the time I hit the staircase, I was crying like a little bitch. Running across the store like said manic was still hot on my heels, I hit the managers' office, only to find the perpetrator... MY FUCKING BOSS. What kind of a SICK FUCK does something like that?!? Needless to say, an epic brawl ensued.

Now, this is before barcodes were invented, and just price stickers were stuck on merchandise, so customers would just basically rip them off one item, and stick them on something else! A $.50 apple sticker would now be stuck on a $200 vacuum cleaner! Oh, the Shenanigans! The Loss Prevention Team was completely useless around there!

<u>Reason for Departure:</u> This place ended going under. Now, this is what I think happened. Aside from store losses due to security oversite, the owner was getting older, and had three irresponsible children who would have eventually tanked this place anyway, so he basically decided to beat them to the punchline! He did it on purpose!

# Chapter 3

<u>RCA</u> This stands for Radio Corporation of America, but if you worked there, you would think it was really an acronym for the Relatively Conscious Association, Really Crushed Associates, or Retarded Customer Affiliation. If you ever have had the opportunity to ever be employed in a union based company, the experience is indescribable. Seriously. It's like following Alice down the rabbit hole. COMPLETE LAWLESSNESS with no sense of repercussions ANYWHERE. ANYHOW. It's basically like giving a bunch of ill motivated monkeys a hand grenade. I'm talking sex in the parking lots, illicit drugs being consumed in the bathrooms; pretty much like a Candyland of horrific debauchery probably only comparable to the ancient Greeks…and, in my personal opinion, perhaps surpassed. Strangely, though, every product that was shipped from this factory had a quality control perfection rate of 99.9% at any given time of receivement from our recipients…go figure.

At this particular place my job was to load 30 pound funnels for the backs of TV's on a conveyor line, on every other hook that went by. The person on the other side would load the remaining. These funnels were shipped packed four in a box, four boxes wide, 8 high, and were loaded by forklifts from the delivery trucks through a hole in a platform where they could be brought up when needed. Loading the line was hard enough, but then the boxes had to be collapsed and put on pallets, the separators had to be removed and also placed on pallets, and the chipped ones had to be discarded into a hopper. The line never stopped moving. EVER. This was to be considered THE WORST POSSIBLE department to work in, in the whole building. I was still young and physically fit back then, but I STILL could not load the line on time. Then the guy who was training me offered me the weirdest advice: Try loading the line slower, you'll go faster. I'm serious. I'm like, "What the hell kind of advice is that?!? I can't even keep up NOW!!!" Clearly the voice of logic was completely devoid here, but I did listen to him. And guess what? Good Christ, he was right. The slower I moved, the quicker I became. My loading ability became like a ballerina in some hideous theatrical ballet, choreographed by some demented director. Soon I was able to actually able to read a novel while I was loading. Seriously! All thanks to illogical advice. THANK YOU ILLOGICAL ADVICE EVERYWHERE!!!

Which is what brings me to my next segment of total weirdness. As mentioned earlier, this company was a complete playground for total personal and moral destruction, so everyone was basically a complete glorified babysitter for those lost souls of partiers, that would, in turn, babysit the babysitters. Clearly, this was a vicious cycle, which strangely, managed to work in some kind of efficient symbiotic nature.

This is a story that, "It's funny now that nobody got hurt" rings true like a Clarion call. Dealing with deviants, you just assume the worst case scenario, which is why when Russ was working with me, and soon became undeniably mysterious, I just assumedly chalked it up to a little, "break time relief." He managed to launch himself on top of the glass funnel delivery; his only saving grace being of smaller stature, or his antics would have brought him to an untimely end, full of shattered glass and clearly a lot of explaining and paperwork to do by upper management. Thinking that he was just all twisted up on something, I was thankfully efficient enough to run both sides of the line, WHILE TRYING TO DISLODGE HIM AND NOT ACCIDENTALLY KILL HIM AND NOT ALERT ANY UNWANTED ATTENTION AT THE SAME TIME! What a feat! I finally send this guy out on break when I felt that some kind of semblance of coherency finally settled in. He comes back totally normal, and I'm still wondering what he quite possibly have taken that would, in layman's terms, "absolutely screw him up that bad with such a short recovery time." Turns out, the poor kid was a diabetic. People, please do not be ashamed if you have issues. Please tell your coworkers. No one is very judgmental nowadays. He could've died over telling me he just needed a candy bar or a shot out of his locker. PEOPLE GET YOUR SHIT TOGETHER!

At the same time, this guy I used to work with used to run this football pool, but although an incredibly hard worker, he just basically got tired of doing it, so he told me that he would give me 10% of the profits, if I would just do it for him! Some days I would be running the line AND counting out about a grand while doing it! Boy, was I the little entrepreneur and multitasker! I was not only saving fellow employees, but I was also making extra money while working! I just had to turn the fans off for a bit, because none of that green confetti needed to end up in a tornado spewed out onto the floor!

## Terrible Things Involving This Company Sending Me to School

Now, at the same time, this company would send you to any college for free! Your choice of study didn't even have to be job related, either! You could go for astrophysics or astrology, they didn't care! So I chose to go to Merrywood in between working double shifts to go for a Bachelor's Degree in Illustration. This was really great because I didn't have to pay for my education, but I ended up spending all of my break time at work either writing papers or sleeping with my head in the ladies' room sink. What a trade off!

Now, this was a religious school. (I know, what was I doing there?) But we were required to take three religion classes. This is weird because all the priests and nuns would not be dressed in their normal garb. They would just be dressed like regular civilians! This meant walking through the busy hallways and trying not to curse because I was overtired, pissed off, and carrying a shitload of books with me. I never knew who was who!

Class #1 This is how I got thrown out of my first religion class. (Imagine that!!!) The teacher was a super, cool priest that asked the class to write a three page paper on why we either did or did not believe in God. Well, I ended writing a 10 page manifesto on why I didn't believe in God. I wasn't being vindictive or mean, but I thought I was quite eloquent. Part of my paper said that worship was like a garden. God was like the Sun, and all the rose bushes and the other plants needed him to grow! But, maybe, someone, somewhere could be a mushroom! They didn't need the Sun like the rose bushes did, and maybe they weren't as pretty, but they still did their job in the garden! They might hide from the light behind a tree, but they still maintained the place!

This is where the priest asked me to stay after class one day. Now, I am thinking I am going to get screamed at! I approach his desk with terrible trepidation, and he says to me, "I read your paper." "OK," I say, completely in utter terror. OH GOD, I WAS GOING TO HELL RIDING A DONKEY OR A SLOW MOVING RIDING LAWN MOWER! "I just want to tell you that this was the best paper I've ever read!" he exclaimed with delight! "But I said I didn't believe in God!" I say! "Do you know how many fucking, stupid, bullshit papers that I have had to read over the years?!? It's been horrible! Can I keep this? This is what I have been trying to teach to these mindless kids, TO THINK FOR THEMSELVES!" Wow, this was weird coming from a priest! Still, though, I was locked into some semblance of religious immobilized terror! Then he says the weirdest thing ever to me." "I would really not rather you attend my class anymore, but you have an 'A' for the semester. I would actually be embarrassed to teach this class in front of you". Thinking that this was some kind of trap, (him failing me for nonattendance) I still showed up for a few more classes, until I think general laziness set in, and I stopped showing up altogether. But this man of the cloth was true to his word! I did indeed receive an 'A' for the semester! See, not all priests are bad!

Class #2. This brings me to the story of the nun. I was very overtired at the time, so every time that I would have to write a paper for anything, I would just basically plagiarize my text books, ripping off random material. So one day after class, this nun asks me to stay. OH, GOD, NOT AGAIN! After everyone left, she says she wants to talk to me about my papers! Thinking that she had noticed that I had rewrote half of them from my books, I approached her in absolute terror! Then she says the oddest thing to me! She tells me that these were the best papers that she has ever read and asks me if I would mind if she could publish them. Knowing that I had stolen all of the material, and that someone, someplace, would eventually notice this, I say, "Um, I really don't know if I feel comfortable with that." But, here was the really creepy part. She was from Italy, and everyone knows people from Europe are VERY close talkers! So as I am speaking with her, she starts getting closer, and closer AND EVEN MORE CLOSER TO MY FACE! Now I am leaning against a desk in some kind of crazy yoga stance, WHILE THIS NUN IS AN INCH AWAY FROM MY FACE!

I finally escape to my next class, where I tell my cool professor that I am pretty sure that Sister Theresa tried to kiss me! "That is fucking awesome!" he exclaims! "NO, IT

WASN'T! IT WAS LIKE TERRIBLE MENTAL RAPE!" I scream back! "I WAS TRAPPED, AND COULDN'T ESCAPE!" "HA HA HA!" he rolls laughing. So this is how dissention was handled at this shanty place! Well, this was the funny part. A few weeks later, the professor grabs me, and says he has the weirdest news! Sister Theresa turned out to be a lesbian, and ran off with another nun to Italy! (Apparently, that was great place to retire if you were a gay nun couple!) I was right after all!!!

Class #3. I now I had to take a marriage counseling class given by an eighty year old nun. There were so many things wrong with this scenario, I actually don't even know where to begin. First of all, there was an eighty year old nun giving advice on marriage. I'm not really sure what her previous life was before she joined the Sisterhood. Maybe she was once married and was so miserable that this was the career she decided to delve into! Good for her! Secondly, hearing an eighty year old nun talk about sex is traumatizing. Thirdly, hearing an eighty year old nun talk about sex IS FUCKING TRAUMATIZING! DID I FORGET ABOUT THE TRAUMATIZING PART?!? A small part of me just wanted to crawl under my desk and die of shame or hide with my hands over my head, like they used to show on those old black and white videos entitled "What Should Schoolchildren Do in Case of a Nuclear Attack?!?" What was wrong at this university?!? At least this teacher didn't try to kiss me! Oh, such a saving grace! But she did have one funny story, though. She said that on your first year of marriage, you should get a mason jar and put a penny in it every time you make love. Then, the second year, every time you make love, you take a penny out. "You will always have extra pennies left by the second year, trust me!" No truer words have ever been spoken! This lady was then cool by me. Even if I did hear her say penis!

Here was the most terrible aspect of this place, though. It taught me a very valuable lesson in life. ALWAYS REPEATEDLY SAVE A COPY ONCE EVERY 20 MINUTES OF ANYTHING YOU DO ON YOUR COMPUTER! Because the ones in our lab room would shit the bed constantly! This was a MAJOR university that had THE WORST computer equipment thought possible! How could we all be paying so much for our credits, and have to deal with such bullshit?!? Seriously, an Etch A Sketch would have more capabilities! Some poor student would spend three hours working on a project, and then suddenly the computer would just inexplicably shut off, losing everything, leaving this poor, suicidal individual shrieking, "OH MY GOD! I AM GOING TO FUCKING KILL MYSELF!" These declarations would reverberate from the downstairs, all the way up to the second floor, where our classes were going on! Knowing what had happened, and being equally sympathetic, we would all cry out in unison, "That poor bastard!!!"

After the second time that this happened to me, I came up with a great idea! (Now, keep in mind that this was before laptops and tab drives were invented. We might have well as tried and invented the fucking wheel at this point!) So I start taking my tower to school. Aside from carrying all my text books, I now have to drag that daunting piece of circuitry, too! Suddenly, Merrywood wasn't so very merry anymore!

Anyways, I ended up graduating Summa Cum Laude from this university. I think that is Latin for, "I Tried to Pretend that Nothing Ever Happened Here." Then worse things started to occur ...

Now this company came out with this great idea to buy stocks with them. You would only have to have so much taken out of your paycheck every week. I always was looking for a way to make extra money, so this sounded like a wonderful opportunity for me! But here was the catch, you couldn't trade or sell anything within three years. That was OK with me, because I thought I would be working there until retirement, but apparently, NO! But they just kept on splitting and splitting! At one point, I was up to $400,000.00. Yeah! Go, Vaness!

Then the ugly factor happened. This company had used everyone's investments to move it down to Mexico! Suddenly, we were all stuck with worthless stocks! I watched in horror as mine declined to $200,000, then to $50,000, then, eventually, to $2,000! "OH, GOD, ALMIGHTY!" And there was ABSOLUTELY NOTHING I could do about it! It was like watching a hostage situation gone horribly awry! (Now RCA stood for Really Conning Americans, to me!) I scream to my stepdad, which was equally stuck in the same predicament as me! So the two of us ended up selling them for pennies! My dreams of a wonderful retirement were absolutely wasted! Still, to this day, if I could find any CEO in this company, I WOULD SHOOT THEM IN THE FACE!!! FUCK YOU, YOU COCKSUCKERS!

<u>Reason for Departure:</u> RCA ended up moving to Mexico. And then China. Fuck them!

# Chapter 4

<u>Various Illicit Employment.</u> At this point in time, I had saved up enough money to buy a house in the country. The only problem was, I signed the papers for it on a Monday and by that Friday, I find out that RCA is leaving the country. I am a single young girl with a mortgage and no job! The NAFTA program at the time offered great benefits, such as: we will send you to a technical school for up to two years for free with unemployment checks. This probably sounds like a great deal, but being able to swing a hammer for one-third of the paycheck for the same amount of hourly labor that you are used to enduring, is a SHITTY DEAL TO ME. I once had a male boss that used to have a saying, "Hold on, at let me put on some lipstick first, because I would at least like to look pretty BEFORE YOU FUCK ME!" Aside from his non politically correct statement during horrific business deals, I had to admit, I agreed with him. The NAFTA program made me feel like I should be applying "Bubble Gum Pink Government Screw Me in High Gloss" at any given day.

I ended up working a myriad of odd jobs to make ends meet. Hence, bartending after my day jobs. This career clearly deserves a novella in itself, which cannot ever be completely be described here. I worked at a seedy place, which was ripe with all walks of life – bikers, hookers, general vagrants, you name it. Strangely, all were good tippers, but general mayhem was assured there at any given weekend. Thankfully, this was before cameras were so en vogue, because some of the bar fights that would occur were incredible! They would usually start out near the present band playing, roll through the dance floor, around the pool table, somehow inexplicably into the restrooms, back out, back around the pool table, through the dance floor once again, and out the front door, leaving any innocent bystander to wonder what possible outcome could have occurred! It was like watching an old Western, but without the six shooters, which why ironically, this place was actually named The Western.

Now, this place had more problems than bar fights. When I was working on slower nights, and standing stationary, I would feel little things run across my feet. Then I noticed the bugs! I asked the owner about it, and he tells me they are river beetles! Well, I'm not an entomologist, but I was thinking cockroaches! So I devise two plans! Plan A was to never stop moving behind the bar, no matter how slow I was! This would keep them off of my feet and legs! Plan B was to come home at the end of a shift, and basically leave my purse in my car, and then strip naked before I went into my house, for fear of dragging any of these nasty critters in there! I certainly didn't need a breeding ground for these creepy things! Although, they were comparably complacent to some of the customers there…

I once saw a girl throw a bottle from about 20 feet across the room and completely nail her boyfriend in the head! This trajectory was so spectacular, it left him out cold on the floor. Thinking that imminent death had occurred, and that I had over served them, I briefly considered cutting my losses, going home and packing, and heading to Mexico incognito. Thank God the recovery time for a 20 mile per hour 16 ounce bottle to the temple of an average male head seems to be around 15 minutes!

Also, I would like to mention my hideous inability to judge age. This is a surely an absolute terrible disability in the bartending industry. Sometimes I would card people in their 40's, but would serve someone that was 15! I once accidentally served the Chief of Police's 17 year old daughter, which when brought to by attention by the owner, caused me to almost have a heart attack and scream, "Oh, fuck! What have I done, AGAIN?!?" Thankfully, she was more into just playing pool than getting loaded, and the owner had connections...

# Chapter 5

Which is how I ended up working for his son installing rain gutters on houses during the day. These were seamless, so it would entail an extreme amount of choreography to install them. A roll of coil stock would be pressed coming out of a trailer usually about 40 or 50 feet long, obviously depending on the length of the house. Then, usually three ladders were set up to the roof tops, and everyone had to pick up their part and carry it up and their drills in sync to install them. If one person made a mistake, the piece would bend, thus ruining it. Strangely, our efficiency was incredible, considering the amount of precision needed and deviants that worked together. It was like being back at RCA, but much more dangerous. Much, MUCH, more.

The ringleader was a chain smoking, crazed ex Vietnam vet that had open heart surgery. He was prone to screaming in Vietnamese curses when provoked, and so thusly appropriately deemed Mr. Crab, which is how I learned such terms in Vietnamese for "Crazy Boy," and, "Everyone get out NOW!" Every day we were greeted by him with, "Good morning, and go fuck yourselves!" Strangely, Mr. Crab was actually calming to work with and an EXTREMELY excellent carpenter. I learned a lot from him, and he was very patient in an odd way.

Little Billy was the smallest built guy I have even seen (with the exception of Little Kevin). This apparently gave him the ability to defy the laws of gravity. He would actually get on a Victorian rooftop, lean over, hold himself up upside down from falling like a bat, grab the gutter, and screw it in! One day we were working on a garage rooftop when he says, "I don't have time for this ladder shit," and proceeds to walk right off the edge! He lands on his feet like a cat, and proceeds to go into the trailer for another rechargeable battery for his drill like it was a natural occurrence!

Gramps worked with me on a shingling job, which is a completely illogical nickname, considering he was a younger guy. Now, I'm smaller, but a pack of shingles weighs 80 pounds. I can carry one around on the ground, but I have to break them in half to carry up a ladder. The owner's teenage son is on the roof trying to pull a staple out for a half an hour, when Gramps says to him, "Ivan, did you ever think about just killing yourself already? Because I've just watched a girl haul shingles up here ALL GOD DAMNED DAY LONG!" Seriously. How much more of this bullshit could one person endure? Gutters by day, bartending at night, with no hope of reprieve for a girl with a mortgage and two college degrees, which was going nowhere fast, until...

# Chapter 6

<u>American Ass Fault.</u> One night a guy comes in the bar, and proceeds to tell me that if I wasn't such a bitch, he would tip me better. Whereas I proceeded to tell him, that maybe if I wasn't working two jobs, I'd be in a better mood. So he makes me an offer. (And, no, not pimping myself out, either...surprisingly)! He could solve all of my problems! Was there a magic wand involved? How would I like how to learn how to run heavy equipment? The pay was good, and the overtime was even better! Utter confusion ensured on my part! Those big yellow machines on the side of the road? Me? I've never even learned how to parallel park, for Christ Sakes! I never had to even do it for my driver's test! I live in the country, where we basically leave our vehicles anyplace, anywhere!

A myriad of disastrous scenarios went through my head. Basically, upmost and foremost, being not able to master this profession and therefore losing my house! However, I ended up quitting my jobs and taking him up on his offer. Thanks to a great trainer and a brand new articulate truck, I actually managed to master this trade! I ended up working in a landfill in Tellher, PA. Now this experience is not what you are thinking…at all. Landfills are actually exceptionally clean, well maintained, scenic places, probably contrary to popular belief. There were two mountains there. The first one was the quarry where we would mine the stone. This is where my newly honed skills of both backing up to a crusher and under excavators were refined. The other mountain was where the landfill was located and run by Waste Management. Which I would personally like to refer to as Wasted Management. At night we would take the stone that we had crushed during the day and haul it over to the landfill side to cover the garbage.

Which leads me to my favorite dozer operator there, Tommy Sapolis. There were hundreds of garbage trucks that would empty daily from Pennsylvania and New Jersey. One day I hear on the CB that some guy accidentally cuts his finger off from a tailgate swinging shut. Tommy, being the compassionate gent that he is, screams, "Don't worry, buddy, I'm coming over and calling an ambulance!" This guy, terrified and clearly without a Green Card, is like, "I'm leaving NOW!" An argument ensues over the CB over the man's overall wellbeing with finally concluding with Tommy shrieking, "FINE! You leave if you want, but you had better find that finger and take it with you, asshole, because I am not shoveling my tracks tonight and fucking finding it there!" The guy just left, one digit less!

Tommy's undying compassion didn't end there, though! There were chain link fences set up to keep the garbage from blowing around. Tommy sees a kitten caught in it one day, rescues it, and puts it in his dozer. Obviously scared and disorientated by its captivity in such a terrifying piece of machinery, (much probably like my opinion on my training), it does the only thing that it is capable of. In it's inconceivable terror, it bites him. Tommy just shrugged it off, but he unfortunately made the mistake of mentioning something about the incident on the CB, which upper management overheard. He ends up giving the kitten to one of the haulers that we knew, but when he went to punch out that night, epic travesty ensued! Upper management wanted to know where that feline was! They were concerned about rabies, and, much like the Red Queen, were like, OFF WITH ITS HEAD!!! When faced with losing his job, Tommy did the most plausible action available to save the cat's life, he lied – he said he couldn't remember what truck he gave it to. This lead to an ultimatum of either a threat of a job loss of 18 years or a series of rabies, distemper, and tetanus shots. Tommy took the latter.

<u>Lesson learned:</u> DON'T BE A NICE PERSON.

<u>Reason for departure:</u> Company's contract untimely ended.

# Chapter 7

<u>My Mona Trucking.</u> They had an operation subcontracting to Rigatoni Excavators off of Rt. 33 in Staulkertown. They were nice enough to give us a company car, a Subaru. So the three of us operators would meet in Dunmore everyday, for an hour and a half ride each way. Now, I have always had a problem will narcolepsy in a moving vehicle. Seriously. Someone turns the key, and I'm out like a canary with a blanket over its cage, so I would always be shoved into the backseat. Tony had, like, 8 children and, suffering from sleep deprivation, only to be rivaled with some kind of depraved Nazi experiment, would ride shotgun. Sean, strangely having his license revoked, would insist on driving, despite being totally and completely illegal. Unfortunately, on this particular morning, Sean had clearly spent the previous evening imbibing into the late hours of it. So when the disaster occurred, it was a miracle that no one was ever injured or even killed. All three of us managed to fall asleep going down Rt. 33. Yes, this is completely true! Thank God it was about 5 in the morning, and traffic was light. BOOM! Right over the median! BOOM! There goes the front tire! And there, hence fore, goes the steering! The three of us wake up screaming! Sean finally gets the

car under control and stopped. All of us were suddenly speechless. What? WHAT?!? WHAT THE FUCK HAD JUST HAPPENED?!? After collecting ourselves to whatever degree thought possible, we were reduced to calling the loader operator from Hiccups, and begging him to sneak out of the quarry with the company's utility truck for assistance. Chivalry at its finest!

<u>Lesson learned:</u> Still to this day, I have no clue. Really. Up the caffeine intake?

Also, on a much related note, Sean and I HATED each other. One day after the incident, when I was too traumatized to nod off, we start screaming about that day's production. I start screaming, "I HOPE YOU GET PULLED OVER, YOU FUCKER, BECAUSE I AM GOING TO SMASH MY FACE OFF THIS DOOR PANEL, AND WHEN THE OFFICER ASKS WHAT HAPPENED, I'M GOING TO TELL HIM THAT YOU FUCKING HIT ME, ASSHOLE!!!" Suddenly, he gets very quiet for a while, the gears and levers of his mind rustily turning, and then proceeds to tell me that I am ONE SICK FUCK! GOOD!!! Never could a better compliment be uttered!

Now, oneday, a blizzard hits the area, and although this company was good enough to give us a car, they were cheap in other ways. We were completely trapped working down there, because traffic was stuck for miles for endless hours. Power was out everywhere, so we finally find an exit ramp and a motel that would take us in. The only problem was, was that this company would only pay for ONE room with only ONE king sized bed! So I end up sleeping between the much hated Sean and an excavator operator. I was sober, because all the bars were shut down due to the electrical shortage, and this, combined with the fact of having to sleep with two strange men, made me explosively enraged! I start screaming, "I SWEAR TO FUCKING GOD, THE FIRST DICK THAT TOUCHES ME IS GETTING RIPPED OFF!" Instead of this being some men's porno dream, they both shriek in unison, "Shut up, Vaness! Just go to bed already!" And that's what exactly happened! Suddenly, my narcolepsy managed to wear off on everyone, much rivaling the Subaru episode! Everyone clocked out instantaneously.

I awoke in the morning, to the weirdest scene imaginable! My makeup was all over the pillow, Sean was drooling on my hair, and the operator's hand was stuck to my face like that terrible creature from the Alien's movie! (That's probably why I woke up; I just couldn't breathe!) Well, apparently my powers of sleepiness work exponentially in reverse, because, immediately they both wake up screaming! It was like some terrible flashback from the Subaru accident! Sean goes rolling off one side of the bed and knocks his head off of the bed stand. (Oh, that's too bad.) But then the other poor guy ends up flipping off the other side and crashes onto the floor, too! By now, I am laughing so bad, I think that I'm actually going to have a rupture! "Shut up, Vaness!" was once again screamed by both!

By now, the harsh reality of the gravity of the situation had set in. The power was still out, so none of us could even take a shower. So we all end up sitting on the end of the bed wearing the same filthy clothing as the day before, screaming insults at each other. Things like, "This really blows!" "I hope you both get run over by a loader!" and "I wish I had a toothbrush, because I would use it down by the river to clean my teeth, and then take it back here, and then shiv you two in the throat with it!" Boy, was that a long day at the office.

<u>Reason for departure:</u> I was hired by Rigatoni Excavators and was sick of working for a cheap ass company that made me sleep with other men!

# Chapter 8

Rigatoni Excavators. This company was run jointly by three brothers. Greg ran the trucking side - tankers and triaxles. Pat ran the excavation side. And Mike sold out, just not generally giving a shit about being concerned with upper management, probably reasonably so. I was not so familiar with Greg, but all three were INCREDIBLY hard workers putting in long hours, much like the rest of us. However, Pat and Mike were also INCREDIBLY hard partiers. Hey, the way I see it, you work hard, you play hard. This lead to their job policy of no drug testing, which in turn lead to complete anarchy and total lawlessness among personnel. I am actually a complete advocate against any testing whatsoever, because, much like the RCA example earlier, I have had the experience to work with people that were much more conscientious and efficient at performing their jobs twisted up out of their minds, than people that were actually sober. Also, it makes for a much more amusing jobsite during a long day.

Our top offender was Al. Pat would let me come in to the quarry at 4:00 in the morning to grease the machines for extra overtime. This meant having the arduous task of trying to find a hundred grease fittings in the dark. On any given weekend, my two-way would go off upon arrival, and Al would say, "Dude, I just got out of the club! I am in Truck 3. Wake me up when the shift starts!" So aside from maintenance, I am now a glorified alarm clock!

On one Sunday, when we were all particularly overtired from working 7 days a week, Al decides to do penance for his actions and get us all coffees that were delivered by… a stripper. She gets in his haul truck to deliver them, when Mike calls me screaming, "Is there a God damn stripper in Al's haul truck?!?" To which I did my best to put the Vulcan mindbend on him. I told him that even though the young woman was attractive and indeed scantily clad, I thought he was being very judgmental about labeling her as a sensual performer. Well, that was the end of her rounds! Still to this day, I wonder how she managed to climb up the haul truck ladder in those platform shoes holding those coffees. Ah, the unanswerable mysteries of the unknown!

Also, Mike was the last person to point the proverbial finger. He had a weakness for the Apocalypse Club on Friday nights, which in turn, lead to one disastrous Saturday. He was unusually late, about a half an hour. Pat calls me screaming looking for him, so being a terrible liar, I was faced with using the usual excuses for covering: 1.) It's dark, and I can't see anything. 2.) I'm in a different part of the quarry. I don't know where the hell anyone is at. 3.) I just drive the truck around here. How long could I possibly stall for this man? My lies were as transparent as single pane glass on a sunny day!

I could see across excavation when Mike finally graced us with his presence, which considering his present inebriated condition, was far from graceful. He gets up on the tracks of the machine to open the cab door and is still so crushed from the night before, takes a header off the side onto the ground. Thinking that his head is smashed like an overripe Halloween pumpkin, I come tearing across the excavation site in terror only to find out that God really does protect little children and fools. Upon assistance, Mike offers me $50 to get him a V8 and breakfast sandwiches for everyone in the hopes to soak up whatever residual alcohol in his system, so I place the order in the downtown diner. By this point, Pat shows up, madder than a wet hen. The chances of me escaping for the hangover cure were futile! A parked articulate truck is an easy mark!

So I find the dozer operator, Marvin, and ask him to run for it. This proved to be an equally worthless endeavor! Marvin had taken so much acid, that when asked to go, he started shrieking that he couldn't leave his dozer BECAUSE ALL THE ROCKS HAD FACES IN THEM!!! Mother... Of...God! Was there any personnel working there that on that given day that could possibly operate with the guise of normalcy, I wondered? Clearly only one. Guess who ended up hiding their machine and thanklessly retrieving breakfast that morning? Never had so much effort resulted in so little outcome or gratitude.

Now one day Mike calls me and tells me that a goat is watching him from a highwall. How much dope had this man managed to smoke? Where would this goat manage to come from? I started to wonder, because this went on for months! THERE IS A GOAT WATCHING ME! Everday I had to hear about this frigging goat! Which finally lead me to ask the quarry manager, "What's with this phantom goat!?!" I scream! "There IS a goat! It's like a ghost! He lives on the ridges." he says. Great, now I am working with another bunch of deviants and Ghost Goat! Then one day, I finally see this elusive unicorn! Now he is watching ME work! Jesus, did I just smoke dope, too? This lead me to ponder a few things. How did this goat not manage to fall off of the highwall? What was it even eating? There's nothing in a quarry but stone! Was it lonely? Should someone call animal control to take it away to some sanctuary? (Jesus, DID I just accidentally inhale Mike's second hand twisted cigarette?) Which leads me to the next offender, Scotty.

Scotty loved his crystal meth. Now, this is a complete anomaly, because usually when people do speedy drugs, they lose weight. Well, not Scotty, apparently. The more he did, the heavier he got. He was an EXCELLENT excavator operator by all means, but him fitting in the cab of the machine was the equivalent of trying to fit 10 pounds of shit in a 5 pound bag. His ability to even manipulate the controls in such tight captivity was astounding! Unfortunately, he would go on benders for days, thus making him pass out in the machine at work. Now, once again, like RCA, everyone always covered for everyone else, so calling him in Pig Latin on the CB to wake him up was out of the question, and no one wanted to blow their horns in fear that he would either be startled and flip his machine over the embankment or swing his boom, crushing any truck in the immediate vicinity. So my job became to leave my truck, basically rappel up the embankment that his machine was stationed on, and gently rap on the door in the hopes of waking Sleeping Beauty without utter chaos ensuing. This was the equivalent of going to a fancy Japanese restaurant, finding an aquarium filled with exotic fish, tapping on the glass, AND SCARING THE SHIT OUT OF THEM! On occasion, there would be vultures circling his machine overhead, and I would pray that they didn't sense an overdose! Scotty fortunately had the constitution of a cockroach, and, although a physical train wreck, managed to survive. Studies should be done on this specimen!

On third shift, triaxles would load the clinker silo with material that would be eventually become cement. Unfortunately, left to their own devices without supervision, most of the drivers would basically just get hammered. Go third shift! One night, one of the drivers forgets to put his box down after dumping and ends up tearing off the major conveyor line running into the storage facility! A welding company had to be called in at 3:00 A.M. to resurrect this fallen beast of technological machinery!

Eventually, Pat ended up having to apply mandatory drug testing because of the innumerable employee Shenanigans. Which why hiring Mark was both a bane and a blessing. He was a sober driver, so every time someone would have an accident or a random test would occur, Mark would get sent to the lab. Having to go at least once a week, he could've probably driven the route blindfolded. When questioning upper management, he was basically told, SHUT THE

HELL UP! He basically did, because HE WAS THE WORST DRIVER THERE, and his only redeeming value was to take one for the team! He would manage to blow out a $5,000 tire at LEAST once every six weeks! But that wasn't, by far, his worst offense!

When you work excruciating hours, everyone needs to amuse themselves somehow. So every Porta-John on any given level of the quarry was stocked with porn. Now, one would think this would offend a woman, but after numerous classes drawing naked people at Merrywood, I have been completely desensitized to any act involving nudity. So, my job as a hauler, would be to circulate the material from these erotic libraries to all the other stationary operators. Who wants "Babysitters with Big Tits" today? How about "Bedroom Amusement Park"? Then one day, the unthinkable happened. ALL THE PORN EVERYWHERE WENT MISSING. A TERRIBLE AND UNHOLY CRISIS! What could've possibly happened? Aliens? An act of God? WHAT?!? Mayhem ensued! After various screaming due to possible sexual withdrawal and phone calls were made, the culprit was apprehended – that dickhead, Mark! WHY, you might ask? Because his girlfriend was offended by such material. Was she presently employed or considering possible employment at this company?!? NO!! So then WHAT THE FUCK?!? Put your skirt on and go home, bitch!

Lesson learned: Don't hire a cunt!

Honorable mentions for Stupidity are now presented to… the Water Truck Driver at Hiccups. All the workers there hated us because they were union, and we were not. We weren't scab workers, we were working there because they simply did not have enough of the manpower or the type of equipment necessary to perform the act of removing the overburden (crap dirt that is basically in the way and useless).

I am assuming this accident was not of malevolent intent, though perhaps questionable. Water trucks are used to sprinkle down the dust on these roads. Everyone that drove haul trucks would park in an area on top, and the operators that ran track machines that were inefficient to escape the bottom hole would drive their pickup trucks down there and park next to their machinery. One day, the water truck driver from Hiccups goes to back up under the water tower, AND HITS A FUCKING LEG ON IT!!! This whole thing goes over ass over tin cups and lands directly on Mike's pickup, crushing it like a pancake! There was not even a prayer of towing this thing out! This poor innocent victim of malice made its untimely departure in life by being unceremoniously scooped up by a loader bucket and thrown on a roll back, and much like an unappreciated dead whore, was sent off to Valhalla to be buried in the Vast Kingdom of Junkyards.

<u>Lesson learned:</u> Beware of resentful union workers!

<u>Another Honorable Mention for Stupidity</u>…Myself. That's right! I am an honest person, and will admit it when I screw up, even hardcore. This is a tale on how I learned to run an excavator. (Strangely, I was actually dead sober when this incident happened…surprisingly.) I was so happy to get hired by this company, that I would detail the insides

of the machines after the day shifts left, while refueling them out of a stationary tank. The only problem was, the nozzle on this particular unit didn't have an automatic shut-off valve, which was alright by me, because I would time everything in my head. (Note to self, this is a terrible idea.) I was just in the midst of Armor Alling the dashboard in an excavator, when I heard what I thought was the sound of rainfall. CLEARLY, IT WAS NOT! Apparently, that particular machine was not run as much as I thought it was that day, thus requiring about half as much fuel as it regularly did. Now, the fuel tank was on the top, so by the time I managed to run and shut the pump off, diesel fuel was EVERYWHERE! On the top, over the sides of the cab, on the tracks, and onto the ground, somewhat resembling a small retention pond. Now gas can be dealt with (as long as there are no open flames), but diesel fuel IS A WHOLE NOTHER ANIMAL! It stinks, and is impossible to remove, which is why I did the only plausible thing possible…I sat down and had a good cry for an hour!

After somewhat collecting myself, I came up with a plan of action! Clean the machine (with no facilities available) and then dig a hole to bury the spill! This would have been a great option had I A.) Known how to run an excavator, or B.) KNOWN HOW TO RUN A FUCKING EXCAVATOR! These machines were huge, and trying to operate one was like trying to make love to a woman. What are you doing? Where the hell was the instruction manual? I guess I'm doing this the right way if nothing gets broken! Which was pretty much my mantra on digging the Hole of Salvation. After cleaning up the machine as much as possible under the circumstances given, and burying the Pirate's Secret Treasure, I made my great escape. Thankfully the operator of it the next day was a heavy chain smoker, and had absolutely no olfactory senses left in his head!

<u>Lesson learned:</u> Try not to go that extra mile for your job!

<u>The next Honorable Mention for Stupidity</u>... goes to ME! ONCE AGAIN!!! YES! But not completely! When Pat first bought these haul trucks, they were literally BRAND NEW! There was still plastic on the seats and cardboard on the floors, so on my second day, when I almost wrecked one, I would have rather killed myself. We were dumping overburden onto a pond, which is a bad idea in itself, because everything is unstabilized. Secondly, when drivers dump off, the rule of thumb is to never dump parallel to any embankment. Always back up perpendicular, folks! Always! In case of a substance collapse, you have a better chance of survival! Just try and pull forward instead of rolling off the embankment sideways. Well, on this particular day, the particular dozer operator thought it would be a particularly good idea to dump off all in one track! I go to dump off and see my box wobbling. So I dropped it, fully loaded, and pulled forward, in the futile hopes that this would correct the problem...which unfortunately MADE THINGS EXPONTENTIONALLY WORSE! OH, FUCK ALL, NOW THE WHOLE BRAND NEW TRUCK IS READY TO ROLL OFF!

Now people, this is where it pays to both be pretty AND have a good head on your shoulders! Ladies, Mabelline is your best friend, trust me! I don't care what a natural beauty you think you are, EVEN IF YOU REALLY ARE! In the most demure way thought possible under the circumstances, I call Pat as calmly as I could, and say, "Um, if I tell you something, will you promise not to get mad?" This is probably an only line uttered to boyfriends by girlfriends whose periods are incredibly late, so in retrospect, I think Pat handled the issue incredibly well. (Hey, I guess, what's a $300,000 insured truck payment to child support any day?) He calmly left the site in his excavator and tracked up to me, holding my machine up with his boom, and walked my truck down the embankment WITHOUT EVEN YELLING ONE TIME!

Lesson learned: Eyeliner and mascara are very important!

This debacle was eventually reciprocated. One day, I'm in excavation. Pat shows up, and tells me to park my haul truck and talk to him. So, as directed by upper management, I do. He proceeds to show me a TERRIBLE rash all over his hands and belly, and asks what it could possibly be. Me, clearly not having any prior medical background, ruled out syphilis, due to the fact that his nose still seemed to be intact. (That was all I was truly capable of.) Then he wanted to tell me something personal, and quietly. Please lean over the truck door to hear it. Now, much like a Brother's Grimm novel, I should've seen this one coming, but what with all the warning signs, no. He precedes to grab me, pull me over the door, AND RUB MY FACE IN HIS FESERTERING RASH ON HIS STOMACH! If you ever thought rape is bad, this was much, MUCH WEIRDER and consequently, strangely terribly worse. Finally, much like an angry badger with rabies, I managed to escape physically, but my dignity was still lost somewhere in that pickup. It turns out that he had poison ivy, which is strange because most women end up catching the clap from their bosses, but I somehow, perhaps being supernaturally blessed, managed to escape both!

<u>Lesson learned:</u> Never trust a whispered secret!

Eventually, the hour and a half commute started to get to me, so I bought a camper and set it up behind Pat's garage. This had its good points and bad points, obviously. In the positive light, the garage was brand new and all the property was surrounded by chain link fencing and lighted at night, so I felt secure. Even the sounds of the Lehigh River directly behind me were soothing. However, in retrospect, the negative aspects unfortunately far out shadowed those positive ones. At the time of the camper purchase, I was blatantly unaware that there were two different types: all season and NOT all season. Apparently, I bought the latter, which made for fresh hell in the wintertime. All the water pipes were on the outside walls, so they would freeze, thus leaving me without showering capabilities. Thankfully, Pat would never lock the garage doors, so I would wait until the young Hispanic crew that would detail the triaxles indoors would leave at night and then stealthily creep into the shop and wash my hair in the wash basin and then proceed to take a Polish shower in the bathroom. (Me being Polish, this is NOT a derogatory remark!) My propane kept running out, so usually I would sleep in the camper, fully clothed for the next day's work. Thank God for high metabolisms!

Occasionally, on extremely frigid nights, I would actually sleep in my truck with it running and the heat on. It probably would have been more efficient to either sleep in the garage or IN ONE OF THE GOD DAMN HAUL TRUCKS LIKE AL USED TO DO!!! You know that you've hit a new low in life when you realize that a junkie has more common sense than yourself!

Now this is a completely terrible chapter in the camper story. If you are unfamiliar with their workings, here is a brief commentary. The plumbing involves two parts. Gray water is the harmless water from your kitchen sink, bathroom sink, and tub/shower area. This can just be let out underneath it to run freely. Thanks Lehigh River! Your toilet system runs to a holding black tank also underneath, so you have two choices: either A.) Call a septic service to empty it out, or B.) Do it yourself. This involves attaching a blue plastic rolling device and hooking it up to a small gate. Pat had a sewage dump off unit there, so, in the hopes of being frugal, I opted for the latter. Being familiar with having a septic system at home, I had no problem with handling this task...UNTIL THE FUCKING EXPLOSION HAPPENED!!! Somehow the camper ended up shifting on its blocks, so the front door would occasionally pop open. Well, apparently that wasn't the only thing to not line up correctly! I go to empty out the tank, AND THE FUCKING GATE WON'T SHUT!!! Gallons of shit come uncontrollably spraying out all over me! OH JESUS, GOD!!! WHY?!? Finally, I get this Feces Demon under control. Sitting there, completely covered in poo, I did the only thing possible. Much mirroring the earlier diesel debacle, I had no choice, but to have a good cry, probably for an equal amount of time. Then I changed clothes, tried to get cleaned up as best as possible, and went shopping for bags of lime! Adding to my trauma, trying to locate this item in Bethtakehim was a real chore!

My understanding is that lye will dissolve a dead body, whereas lime will cover up the eventual stench. The only logic I could come up with was that the area was of high homicidal crime rate, and absolutely no chain of stores wanted to be associated with any such dealings. Finally, I found a seller and after purchasing a multitude of bags, and much like a serial killer wanting to review his horror inflicted, returned to the scene of the crime. Oh, and it was bad. Really bad! Which was how I learned to run a dozer. (Unfortunately, most of my equipment operating education has been based on disaster relief, usually caused by yours truly). Fortunately, though, CAT keys are universal, which means any one will operate an excavator, a loader, or an articulate truck, regardless of any year of manufacture. So, after flailing around helplessly, with God's saving grace, I had managed to get the situation under control before anyone noticed. Never has excrement probably caused a single individual more travesty.

<u>Lesson learned:</u> There is absolutely none, and probably won't be anymore in this book, because the level of logic has been clearly, noticeably been in an increasingly in a downward spiral. Sorry, kids.

Equally elusive as lime in that neighborhood, were apparently library books. Having no access to TV at night and trying to find some way to amuse myself, aside from complete and total deviant behaviors, I tried to better myself. Thinking that the local library would be a good option for a more positive outlet for my creative side, I visited it. I selected a book and upon checkout was told that because I wasn't a resident of that county, I could not be issued a card, and therefore not be able to leave with said book. I calmly tried to explain that I had a house up North, and that surely collateral could be involved, much to no avail. PEOPLE, THIS IS WHAT IS WRONG WITH THIS COUNTRY! I am working out of Bethtakehim near Allenstown, which I could score an 8 Ball of coke on any street corner, BUT I CAN'T TAKE OUT A FUCKING LIBRARY BOOK?!? REALLY?!? Fine! Barnes and Nobles, here I come! Assholes!

<u>Lesson learned:</u> (Ok, here is just one more, but it's not a very good one<u>.)</u> Just do drugs, they are easier to score than books!

Things that were unfortunately not as elusive as library books during my encampment there - river spiders. Now, I'm sure everyone has their terror of everything — mice, snakes, heights, whatever. Well, mine is spiders! Complete unbridled terror would ensue! Living in the county has taught me to deal with the smaller ones. I am actually kind of a compassionate soul, and will use the whole glass jar and envelope action to put them outside…until the river spider invasion! These arachnids are so big, that they DON'T EVEN USE WEBS! I am pretty sure to this day, that a whole troop of them were responsible for the shifting of my camper! BASTARDS! One morning, I was blow-drying my hair in the dark before work, hooked to the outside of the garage (and, no, gypsies everywhere, this is not a good time, nor a good idea) when I could hear a faint sound over the hairdryer…Plop! Plop! Plop! Apparently, these creatures, much working like a construction crew functioning without a supervisor, in tandem, would manage to creep up the walls at night (much like me rappelling up the shanty slopes of Hiccups in the dire hopes of reviving Scotty), in search of prey that would circulate around the lights that were there for security reasons. Either from the something of the Book of Exodus or just because of poor footing on the metal roofing due to the vibrations of my 220 volt Con air hairdryer (Hey, thanks Pat for those triaxle hookups!), an epic shower of spiders was sent down from some Portal from Hell everywhere. And I mean FUCKING EVERYWHERE!!! HOLY FUCKING CHRIST! Listen, people, for a woman to abandon a child is one thing, but not such a loved and cherished possession as your favorite hairdryer, ladies! BUT JESUS, THEY WERE HUGE AND FALLING FUCKING EVERYWHERE! Once again my fight or flight method probably managed to save my life!

Thinking I was the only pussy there, one day I'm in the garage, and the head mechanic starts flipping out. Those creepy eight legged sneaks had somehow managed to infiltrate the garage and get it into the sodium arc lamps there. He blows a fuse, and starts flipping out that spider shit was all over his office phone, calls were not tolerable because of it, and he could only take so much in life! He gets up on one of triaxles with a can of starting fluid and a lighter, and with a burst of flame, COMPLETELY manages to kill any insect probably within a complete one mile radius, strangely without even leaving as so much as a scuff mark on the roof!

What a mechanic! And an exterminator to boot! What wasn't this man capable of? This is why I loved Gabe!

As a side note, the stink bug population that managed to invade my camper was horrific! If you are unaware of what these bugs are, allow me to enlighten you! They are hideous looking, almost like if someone could manage to morph a small dinosaur into a beetle, but they are completely harmless. They don't sting or bite or get into your leftovers (I'm not even sure what they actually really ate), but God forbid you smash one! (I learned my lesson not to do this after bug one!) Upon death, they release a stench of that compared to German mustard gas! I'm not really sure how to describe it. It was like if you combined road kill, a skunk, and week old garbage together and somehow managed to diffuse it through three rooms at high volume! HOW COULD ONE LITTLE BUG MANAGE TO SMELL THAT BAD?!? It was worse than being trapped in an elevator with a guy overdoused with cheap cologne! I tried everything to get rid of these things! Every pesticide imaginable, but nothing would work! (I was probably, slowly killing myself in the process!) I really wouldn't care about them residing there, but at night when I would try and sleep, these little pricks would get stuck buzzing in my hair, landing on my face, or crawling up my arms! AHHH! Why couldn't I be infested with lady bugs?!? They are so much cuter! I ended up sleeping with my head under the covers all summer long! (This strangely seems to solve a lot of problems in life. I'm not really sure why.) Where was Gabe when I needed him?!?

Also, regarding the camper arrangements, after paying rent there, I became Pat's Little Bitch. One night, he calls me at 11 at o'clock telling me that I have to give Gabe a ride to the MAX facility to pick up a tractor there needed for the morning. Now, if you are unfamiliar with these vehicles, most people have the tendency to call them just tractor trailers. This is misleading, because when detached, the truck that does the hauling is called the tractor, and the trailer is basically the hauling device. On our return trip, Gabe two-ways me and asks if I perhaps heard the sound of rain hitting my personal truck. Yes, indeed I did! We pull over, only to discover that a fuel line had blown off the tractor, thus rendering it useless. My truck sat there behind it, pitifully having diesel fuel dripping off the cab, windshield, and hood. ONCE AGAIN ANOTHER DISASTER INVOLVING DIESEL FUEL AND I!!! By the time the dealership mechanic arrived and fixed the problem, it was about 3 in the morning before we got back to the shop. On arriving there looking like two people on an epic four day bender, Gabe hands me the company card, and tells me to wash my truck. Thank God for angels barring company wares! By the time I finished, I had roughly an hour to sleep before dayshift!

Now, at this point, Pat really started the mental abuse. There were two cement plants with which we worked at. With limestone being prevalent in that area, they were in close proximity with each other. Well, Pat, in his efforts to be frugal, did not want to have to pay a lowboy to move the loader in from one to another, so he would repeatedly call me at 2 in the morning to drive it then and there,

IMMEDIATELY! What choice did I have? I was presently stuck under the hellacious reign of His Landlordship Property Owner. I would get stuck picking up and driving this loader in the dark through the town to my, hopefully, achievable destination. Now, this was completely illegal, but in the wintertime, at least there would be an excuse if I was so unfortunate to be pulled over by the police – snow removal for the county! But this was the summertime, and no excuse could be deemed viable! No, officer, not just leaving the bar with this 50 ton monster! Just unexplainably cruising with it – thought I would bring flowers to mom!

Driving illegally through a main thoroughfare, using every mental capacity I had, caused me to try and apply the Cloak of Invisibility to this giant, yellow piece of machinery. Clearly emitting high volumes of mind static paid off, because I never was, but my treacherous journey would not end there. Much to my dismay, the pilgrimage would continue out of town, through woods, over railroad tracks without gates (OH, GOD, TRAIN, PLEASE HAVE YOUR LIGHTS ON!) back into more woods, and into the quarry, where I would park this beast, completely exhausted from my epic physical and mental trek. Pat, YOU DICK!

One night, after an apparently spectacular round of partying, he bursts in my camper. Now, I was dead asleep, so this untimely intrusion SCARED THE HELL OUT OF ME! I burst out of bed, and go hauling ass into the kitchen thinking that invisible robot ninjas were attacking, only to find him standing there. "What the hell happened to your face?!?" he screams. "I DON'T HAVE ANY MAKEUP

ON, YOU ASSHOLE!" I shout back! So, all he wants to do is have a beer with me before he goes home. FINE! So I get him one. He stares at the Filler Light can and says, "You know, I pay you good money here, SO WHAT'S WITH THIS FUCKING SWILL YOU SERVE ME?!?" After my extensive bartending experiences, I calmly asked him if he would like to be wearing it. He slammed it, and much like an unwanted specter in an exorcism, managed to dematerialize into his truck for probably what would be a profound ride home, to usually, I would assume, an exceptionally pissed off housewife!

Another night, he has me drop paperwork off at his office when he was there at his desk. Upon entering, I couldn't help but notice that the door frame was terribly askew and completely destroyed! "Um, I'm not trying to be rude and pry, but what the hell happened to your door, Pat?" I ask. "YOU WOMEN NEED TO GET YOUR GOD DAMN HORMONES IN CHECK! MINNIE JUST RIPPED IT OFF IT'S HINGES ON HER WAY OUT!" (Now I never met Minnie, but I knew that she was a tiny, Hispanic marathon runner who would drive tanker trucks for him. And given Pat's spectacular ability to piss anyone off in a nanosecond, I figured that he probably deserved it!) "Well, what the hell did you do to her?!?" I scream! "Nothing!!!" he shouts back! "Do you know why your eyes are brown? BECAUSE YOU ARE FULL OF SHIT UP TO YOUR HEAD!" I shriek back! Then I throw his paperwork at him! On my way out, I scream, "IF THIS DOOR WASN'T ALREADY BROKEN, I'D BREAK IT AGAIN, YOU DICK!" The last thing I heard him shout, was something about women and their periods! "Good! You deal with that!" I ended up echoing down the hallway!

Pat did have an extremely funny side to him, though. Regardless of the long hours I worked, the about of chain smoking I did, and the unholy amounts of alcohol I consumed, I always was pretty diligent about working out at the 24/7 Gym in the morning, and running along the Lehigh River trails at night when possible. Unfortunately, the more I worked out, the more weight I gained. I went from around 130 to almost up to 150 pounds! This wouldn't sound so bad, but, folks, I was only 5'5" tall! Strangely, I still had a 32 inch waist and an ass that you could bounce a quarter off of! It was like a vicious cycle. The more I worked out, the more weight I gained! I would shower after the morning workout, and then see all the pretty, skinny vixens head out for their morning runs. I needed to secretly monitor these gazelles and figure out what the hell was I doing wrong! Aside from limited dietary habits only involving large amounts of nicotine, I was barely even eating! The only saving grace was that one morning I flip out during work to Pat about my weight.

Being built like a brick shit house, and obviously having no women skills, he says the most strangely endearing thing to me ever. "Vaness, you will NEVER be a skinny woman ever! EVER!...EVER! However, I have come home many a time with lipstick on my collar to my wife with only to face small repercussions, but I will tell you one thing, I WOULD FUCKING FEAR COMING HOME TO YOU IN THAT MANNER!!!" This statement might offend someone women, but to me, it made me feel good about myself. Fuck those antelopes. I might not be as thin as them, but I could beat the shit out of every one of them. However, they, being obviously faster than me, could probably outrun their predator of jealousy. Does anyone have an ashtray around here anywhere? I might be slower, but my endurance is longer! Trust me, I'll get you ALL eventually!

Anyway, this is Pat's best joke ever. One day after a long day of hauling, I go back to the camper, get changed into my running gear, and he bursts in. JESUS, I needed a stronger door! One that could obviously keep out a 250 pound Italian! (I know his name was Patrick, don't ask me.) He asks me for a beverage, and then asks what I am doing. After tossing him some swill, I tell him that I am planning to run the trail along the river to the Frick building. He recoils in horror, and tells me that that is a round trip of a roughly a ten mile jog. And I proceed to tell him that as soon as I finished my beer and cigarette, I was heading out for my romp. He looks at me silently for a full solid minute and then stoically screams, "VANESSA, YOU ARE EVERY COACH'S WORST FUCKING NIGHTMARE!!! DO YOU KNOW THAT?!?" Well, I was a good athlete, because I blew through that course, only to return to the camper for ANOTHER SMOKE AND A BEER! Scotty wasn't the only person employed there with the only inexplicable constitution! But I still laugh about Pat's rant to this day!

This brings me to my stint in instruction there. (Both instruction and construction) Everytime Pat would hire someone new with no experience, he would always throw them in my truck for me to teach. I actually liked doing this, because I remembered how nervous I was when I was first started doing this kind of work, so I wanted to return to favor to someone else! Here was the weird part, though, all these people were always guys, but some of them would go absolutely AWOL on me! I mean absolutely batshit crazy! Now, I'm not really sure what the underlying problem was here, folks. At first, I thought it was the trucks. They are very big, and imposing, but my understanding in life, is that men are attracted to adrenaline rushes like driving around recklessly on fourwheelers or motorcycles or just being enthralled in crazy relationships, so they would be thrilled to run one of these monsters! I thought secondly, that the problem was the size of the quarry. If you are introduced into a little one, they are easy to navigate around, but this place was HUGE, having about 40 different levels, and being 200 feet below sea level! But I would always tell the new potential employees to calm down, and to just ride around with me for the first few days to get a feel for the place. I tried to be as kind as the guy who initially trained me!

One day, I am trying to teach this one guy, when he somehow manages to disengage his seatbelt, and launch himself on top of me screaming, "I can't do this! Take me back to my car!" This was like trying to dislodge a wet, helpless, baby seal off of me! His weight was squishing me, AND I COULDN'T SEE WHERE THE HELL I WAS GOING! "JUST GET OFF ME, ALREADY, BEFORE YOU KILL US BOTH, YOU FUCKING CLOWN, AND I'LL TAKE YOU BACK, OK?!?" I am shrieking! I drive him back to the parking lot, where he manages to dismount from the ladder with the speed and acrobatics of an Olympian Gold gymnast!

The best trainee I ever had was Pat's 10 year old son! It was apparently "Take Your Kid to Work Day!" And now, Pat wants to put his kid in my truck! Now, I do not have any children of my own, and neither does anyone else in my family, so I have absolutely no clue how to act around them! Utter terror ensued on my part! I felt like the baby seal! Whose lap was I supposed to hide on?!? (And particularly, I really wasn't sure if this was legal to have a small child there who was not MSHA certified in a quarry! But he was very tiny, so I figured that if someone important showed up for inspection, that I could jam him under the passenger seat, motionless, with some newspapers over him!) "PUT HIM IN THE EXCAVATOR WITH YOU! HE'S YOUR KID! I AM NOT A BABYSITTER!" I scream to Pat! "THERE'S NO ROOM IN HERE, YOU IDIOT! HE'S GOING IN YOUR TRUCK!" he shrieks back! "YOU'RE GOING TO BE SORRY, I PROMISE!!!" I yell back!

And that's what happened. This poor child gets tossed into my truck, and is subjected to my nonexistent parental capabilities! For the first few hours, I made shitty, lame conversations with him. So then, getting more strangely paranoid about not being able to entertain him, I devise a plan! (Whereas once again, I would like to say that most of my impertinent ideas are absolutely terrible!) I would amuse this small being in some other way! "Do you want to drive this 40 ton haul truck?" I asked. (This is why God probably never graced me with children; none of them would have ever survived!) "Sure!" he says! So I scoot him over into the driver's seat, buckle him up, and start telling him what all the controls were for. Strangely, he caught on better than the seal!

Now, don't get alarmed folks, because I kept him in first gear the whole time, so he was barely creeping along. Also, sitting in the instructor's seat, I could grab the steering wheel or the Kill Switch in a heartbeat! This switch would shut this whole truck down, and lock up everything in it within a nanosecond! The brakes, the dump body, the computer, completely everything! But this little kid, who probably needed a telephone book on the seat to see over the dashboard was doing great! Such youthful determination!

Then his dad calls me and says, "Hey, I've been thinking, this would be a great idea! Maybe you could try and let my son drive that truck around!" (I apparently wasn't the only one with terrible parental skills around that place!) Being the world's worst shittiest liar, it took me a minute to try and compose some kind of semblance of a convincing tale. Then sensing my terror, he says, "Vaness, Vanessa, is my child driving that truck at this very moment?" I was presently at a loss for an excuse, so the best answer I could come up with was, "Um, I'm not really sure. I guess, like, ah maybe?!?" (Way to go Vaness, way to go!)

Instead of being enraged, he is absolutely delighted! "How's he doing?!?" he asks. "Oh, I'll tell you how he is doing!" I say. Then I put the phone against my shoulder, under my ear, and my hands over the kid's ears, and scream, "I'LL TELL YOU HOW HE'S DOING! HE'S DOING

BETTER THAN HALF OF THE FUCKING JERKOFF, ASSHOLE DRIVERS THAT YOU HAVE PRESENTLY WORKING FOR YOU!!! THIS IS WHAT YOU GET FOR ASKING ME TO BABYSIT!!!" This poor kid is now deaf, and still creeping along! "That's incredible!" his dad yells! Actually, it really was, considering the fact that no accidents happened with this boy's age. Accidents happened all the time at this place with seasoned workers! This, however, was the longest day I felt that I have ever spent on a jobsite! Why was this called, "Take Your Child to Work Day," when it suddenly instead turned into, "Take Your Boss's Child to Work Day, Into a Potentially Disastrous Environment?!?" was beyond me!

Now, I'll tell you why I did this. This is how I learned how to drive. Nowadays, you need a car seat for kids almost up to age 12, and everyone needs a helmet while riding a bicycle. Do you know what? FUCK YOU PEOPLE! If you smash your head, and get a concussion, WALK IT THE FUCK OFF!!! You do NOT need to visit the emergency room every time that you have a bleeding cuticle! Anyway, my stepdad used to take me out on country roads when I was little, and ask me if I wanted to drive! "SURE!" I would exclaim with the same amount of enthusiasm as Pat's kid! Then I would pop over onto his lap, and would steer the car for miles. Screw seatbelts! The two of us would be laughing like deranged fools! "Sharp right, kiddo, and I can't help you, because I have a beer one hand and a cigarette in the other!" he would scream! How much fun did I used to have?!? Well, I tried to incorporate that same amount of amusement into everyone else that I had to train driving! Thanks, Daddy, for the fond memories!!!

Now, because I was the best driver there and had the newest truck, not only did I get stuck training new employees, but I also got stuck doing the most heinous of work – like the pipeline! One day, I am backing into the excavator operator in really tight quarters, when he says the unthinkable, "Honey, I am going to have to flip your truck on its side, so make sure that you have your seatbelt on!" Did I just hear that?!? WHAT?!? SERIOUSLY?!?

"I swear to God, that if you scratch this paint job, or smash one of these mirrors, I will break every bone in your body before Pat gets a chance to!" I scream! (I was incredibly attached to this truck!) "Don't worry, you'll both be OK!" he says, and I believed him, because he was the best operator that I have ever had the pleasure to work with! So he gently lays my truck over, but this is where the trouble started! I am hanging out of my seat, when gravitational forces continued to ensue! My truck turned into some swirling vortex of a random avalanche of shit hitting me in the head! I was belted with assorted things such as my morning coffee, a crossword book, assorted pens and pencils, paperwork for that week, my lunch, the fire extinguisher, a small tool box, the owner's manual, clothing, and strangely, I think, a Rubix Cube and inexplicably, a lawn chair, and someone's luggage destined for Indonesia! Then he finally stands my truck upright, sending this tidal wave of crap back the other way! OH GOD, NO!!! Such devastation!

Speaking of devastation, I felt really bad for the farmers around there, because the water table combined with the limestone deposits from the quarry managed to create huge sink holes in their fields. And I'm not talking little holes, either, I MEAN YOU COULD LOSE A WHOLE VILLAGE IN ONE! Imagine being one of these poor famers there, running your combine and almost flipping it into one of these portholes to hell! I would get sent out to fill these things in, but my truck's windshield was only as tall as the cornstalks, so I could never properly see where I was going. (Much like the farmers!) So I had to totally rely on the quarry manger to tell me where I was going on my phone! "Go left for fifty yards, then go right for another 90, then go left again for another 40!" he would say! This was easier said than done, because all kinds of vegetation matter, like leaves and corn, would be smacking off my windshield, and this was not including the unidentifiable assortment of insects! Then, suddenly, I would almost tumble into one of these pitfalls! The repeated return trips weren't as bad, because I could motor around following my already crushed trails through these deranged mazes of maize! This sucked worse than having seals land on me during training sessions!

This brings me to my snow removal career for Pat. He had a spectacular contract at the Layme Valley Hospital, and I had my large Dodge Ram 2500 diesel. Wanting to earn extra cash, I put a plow on it and an aluminum dump body insert on the back with a tailgate spreader for salt. I would work in the quarry during the day, but when it started snowing, I would get THE CALL! REPORT! REPORT, NOW! Lock and load people! Usually this involved a hellish 48 hour episode of not sleeping, aside from my dayshift routine. This rivaled Tony's sleep deprivation, by far! The only redeeming value was that I was sent out with Mike, who was, "Super Cool" in 80's terminology. By day two, neither of us would be coherent. Which lots were done? What was the score here? Were we still at the hospital? And every year they managed to add on MORE FUCKING PARKING LOTS! PEOPLE STOP GETTING SICK! KEEP YOUR SHIT TOGETHER!!! Tempers were fierce enduring the extensive sleep deprivation!

Now, I adored Mike, but he would have the bad habit of doing absolutely no maintenance on his equipment! But being my favorite Rigatoni, I would always look out for him, so when his gas salt spreader would not start, my job would be to bang on the back of it with rock while he repeatedly tried to start it from the front control box in the cab. This was a terrible decision on my part, because I would be covered in gas and sparks would be flying everywhere. BANG! BANG! BANG! Eventually, much like applying vast amounts of alcohol to a single, lonely woman at any given bar, I would always get this bitch started! (Which one could only assume would lead to an equal amount of banging on that bitch's part!) The only concern of mine was the explosion factor! Which was why when I screamed at Mike one night concerning my general welfare interests, he had the best comeback ever. "Vaness, if destruction happens, WE ARE ALREADY AT A HOSITAL, YOU KNOW, YOU IDIOT?!?" Clearly this man had inarguable and valid points on both of these accounts!

<u>More Honorable Mentions for Stupidity</u>...the people who worked there. Yes, the same people who are probably responsible for being your caretakers THAT APARARENTLY HAVE NO COMMON SENSE! When the weather was inclement at long spans of time, I guess in the interest of safety, some would just leave their cars in the same spot for days. So, in our own interests of safety, no one would plow around them for the fear of sliding and accidentally hitting one. One night a lady comes to eventually retrieve her vehicle, and finding it completely mired in the drifts, starts screaming at a plow truck driver, which he equally returned her rant. "FUCK YOU, YOU FAT FUCKING BITCH! GET A FUCKING SHOVEL AND DIG. IT MIGHT DO YOU SOME FUCKING GOOD!" Did I just hear that?!? (Seriously, did he just even say that?!?) He then proceeds to leave for another parking lot, to probably unleash more unfiltered verbal venom and general mayhem!

Richie was the loader operator there, in charge of scooping up the snow that the plow trucks would push and then flip it over the embankments. Now, Richie had the complacent personality that could probably only be found in a beagle used in experimental testing, so when he got into a fight, I could only wonder what exactly had occurred. Apparently, an owner with a pickup there insisted that he fill his box with snow for weight. Richie politely declined, stating that he could not do it because of insurance regulations. The owner starts really insisting about it and becomes belligerent! Well, so does Richie! My God, what was happening here?

Which leads me to my own episodes of occurrences that should have lead to Anger Management Classes on my behalf. One night I am plowing, and I have half of a huge parking lot cleaned, and head to the other half, whereas this woman proceeds to park in the God Damned snow, which I obviously needed to clean! I drive over and politely suggest to her, perhaps she would be so kind as to move her car over to the area that was already plowed. She proceeds to tell me that she has parked in that same spot for the last twenty years of working there. Now either A.) This woman was a complete nitwit, or B.) This woman was incredibly intelligent with supernatural abilities, and much like a homing pigeon, was able to locate her exact spot under the blanket of five inches of snow! Fine, another mired car, see if I care!

Now, this incident is where, much like Richie's, is when my proverbial fuse blew. One morning, I was heading into a lot, when this car is riding my ass. People are always looking for excuses to sue for money, so even in my sleep deprived state, I subconsciously knew what was happening here. The driver, rather a large and imposing man, gets out of his car, comes running around to my window and starts screaming at me that my salt had damaged his paint job! I calmly let him finish, and then shrieked, "FUCK YOU, AND YOUR 1993 CHEVY CAVALIER! I AM DRIVING A PLOW TRUCK WITH STROBE LIGHTS ON THE TOP, WITH THE DUMP BODY UP, AND IF YOU'RE TOO STUPID TO STAY BACK WITHIN A REASONABLE DISTANCE, FUCK YOU AGAIN! MAY I REITERATE THE SUGGESTION OF YOU GOING

AND FUCKING YOURSELF?!?" Clearly this man was not used to the hormonal and homicidal rage that could only be unleashed by a woman! He gets back in his piece of shit and leaves. I call Pat and tell him to expect a phone call of complaint, which he inevitably did. Any and all involvement on my part of this episode was eventually resolved with basically the hospital telling said driver not to be such a dumb bitch. Case closed!

Probably, the best night plowing, however, was also New Year's Eve. Now, Mother Nature has an obvious disturbed sense of humor. Probably righteously so, considering the fact that no one seems to have ever even seemed to give her the common courtesy or decency of appreciating her spectacular wrath in general, and that of the unparalleled ability to manage TO FUCK UP THE HOLIDAYS! Mike was having a huge a huge party at his house. So when I couldn't make it because of the white stuff, a care package was made and sent out for me – shrimp cocktail and a sippy cup full of Gin and tonic! The occasional job perks!

Reason for departure: Distance.

# Chapter 9

<u>My stint in contracting.</u> I could write whole volumes in this matter, much rivaling a complete set of the Encyclopedia Britannica! Running this business was much like Good the Bad and the Ugly. Installing fencing and porches by day with my present live in boyfriend and doing estimates at night. Never have I missed my sanity or sleep so much in my life!

<u>More Honorable Mentions for Stupidity</u>...Most home owners. Some were just husbands that were trying to appease their wives. Honey, will you stop bitching and/or quite possibly put out tonight if I call for that vinyl fence you wanted so you can let the dogs out in the morning? Clearly these people had no intentions on ever buying anything, EVER! (Fucking tire kickers!) See, dear, I told you we couldn't afford it! Sorry, but thanks for last night! Ya, and about last night, I SPENT HOURS AFTER BUSTING MY ASS ALL DAY IN THE FURNACE OF THE STAR WE CALL THE SUN, DIGGING AND INSTALLING, WORKING ON YOUR FUCKING ESTIMATE, YOU PRICK! Glad YOU had fun!

Others were just plain stupid. We would show up with a pallet of concrete, and ask where the hose was. What hose? We don't have any outdoor running water. What do you need water for? Now, these people managed to own houses and raise families, so I'm not really sure how this confusion could occur in the first place. I'm not a brain surgeon, so clearly I think having an open cranium presented before me, I would be a little apprehensive. However, with the assistance of a good anesthesiologist and the help of my cell phone with You Tube, I would try like hell to give it a go under the limited circumstances, perhaps turning the whole ordeal into a total lobotomy or some kind of deranged Snuff video, BUT I WOULD GIVE IT MY BEST EFFORT, PEOPLE! I'm not an electrician, but I would think it would involve some different gauge wiring and TRYING NOT TO STAND IN OPEN WATER TO AVOID ELECTRCUTION! And I'm not a plumber either, but I'm sure it involves the soldering of copper pipes or PEX hose with clamps. I KNOW WHEN TO STOP TRYING TO IGNITE A PROPANE WATER HEATER AFTER THE FIRST FOUR TRIES! So, folks, how can you and be intelligent enough to pay a mortgage and change a diaper, BUT BE COMPLETELY UNAWARE OF THE FACT THAT CONCRETE NEEDS WATER?!? JESUS, GOD!

<u>The couple from New York.</u> Complete idiots! They had built a slamming house on this lot in the city and wanted a fence installed to not have to see their neighbors' homes in the upper back of them that were older. Fine, but their yard was so flooded that it much resembled the Florida Everglades. Trying to bring equipment through there that was four

wheel drive was almost impossible! Upon installation, we discovered two unfortunate things: A.) There were terra cotta pipes leading underground into their property from their upper neighbors' drainage, and B.) There was a SHIT LOAD of rebar that we were managing to pull from the ground! A whole box of shear pins, completely decimated that day! What the hell was going on here? Then I hear what I think can only be the sound of a toilet incessantly flushing during the day. Who could that be, Casper the Friendly Ghost? No one was even home! Well, it turned out to be the sump pump that apparently ran nonstop. When questioned about this mysterious piece of property, we were told PROUDLY by the owners that they had purchased it at a good price, because it was the borough's machinery scrap dump site! Clearly, we had managed to resurrect most of the fallen mechanical beasts in our efforts of installation! What logic is this, one might wonder? Build a $400,000 house on basically a landfill? Have your two children play on leaking batteries all day? Their answer for their problems they had, was bringing in more dirt! Think drainage people! Some jobs didn't have enough water, AND THIS ONE HAD WAY TO FUCKING MUCH!

<u>Also, lower contenders</u>…Delivery truck drivers. I'm sure these poor bastards were probably only getting paid minimum wage, and considering the fact that they had to probably initially pay for their CDL licenses out of pocket, just really couldn't give a flying fuck at a rolling donut. People would order these "Special Order Fences" and then get pissed off when I would tell them that it would take at least two weeks for delivery. Then the uttermost disaster

would occur! It would arrive on scheduled jobsites only to find boxes of damaged material! So I did the only thing in my power to resolve the issue, I became crafty. After most nights of barely any sleep, I would get up before dawn, and much like a cat and mouse game, catch these jerkoffs unloading their damaged wares! TAKE THIS SHIT BACK, YOU ASSHOLE! DON'T GO LEAVING IT HERE! Many of time was screamed by myself! This in turn would aggravate the customer as to why things were running late. Now they were going to have to wait an additional two weeks! Well, people, let me tell you something, now this was fucking up the schedule on my part! Every job that I had, had to be switched around now! This incorporated ceaseless bitching and whining from other customers, and much like a row of dominos falling over, shit manages to roll downhill!

However, we did manage to meet some wonderful people. A brief list including:

The two gay guys from New York. If you're homophobic, fuck you, because these two gentleman were one of the nicest, most sweetest couples that we had ever worked for. Now, for a couple of let's just say a different lifestyle, I have complete sympathy for them in trying to select a construction company who would not be judgmental. Having social anxiety disorder my whole life, and painfully forced not to be a recluse due to vast amounts uncontrollable environmental factors, the message on my phone's voicemail said in my voice, "Welcome to Vram Construction! Please leave a message, AND DON'T BE SHY!" (You'd laugh, but I actually got a lot of women calling for estimates, because they were nervous and didn't want to deal with men!) Anyway, this wonderful pair had a huge renovated house with a giant garden outback, complete with huge statues and water fountains. They wanted a high fence around it due to their neighbors' issues with their living arrangement. Who wouldn't want a gay couple living next to them?!? Not to stereotype, but usually their houses are well kept and so are their yards! White trash for anyone? No thank you, ma'am! Even my boyfriend, who was a brawny construction worker, said in wonder, "Would you just look at all this?!? It's God Damn spectacular! I love these guys!" We finished the job, and they were so happy that they actually sent photos of their new sanctuary to our house! We still love you gay guys, and your ignorant neighbors can go and fuck themselves! How is that for poetic justice!

<u>The nun.</u> After years of working in the construction trade, I had ABSOLUTELY no filter on my mouth, so I prayed to whatever deity was out there, please don't curse, Vanessa, please, PLEASE, try and maintain your composure! It's completely imperative to customer relations to maintain an act of somewhat of presentable dignity and composure. What if this bride of God had some special telepathic capabilities? Much like the guy in the Village of the Damned movie, I kept thinking brick wall, BRICK WALL! Don't say fuck in your head! Much like a person suddenly conflicted with Tourette's Syndrome, I uncontrollably started to bite my tongue to divert any belligerence on my part.

Well, this woman turned out to be COMPLETELY lovely! We arrive there and she promptly says that she doesn't want to get screwed on price by paying someone that we were subcontracted to. She wanted OUR price and had all the inventory needed already figured out! Perfectly! I had to contend with customers that didn't ever know that we needed water, AND HERE WAS A NUN THAT HAD DONE A FLAWLESS INVENTORY LIST FOR ME JUST TO BE POLITE AND SAVE ME TIME FROM ESTMATING AT NIGHT!

She was completely happy with our work, and managed to stay in touch with me over the years. She told me that her spirit animal was a brown bunny (which secretly I thought it was a little Pagan, but seriously, she was so super cool, who was I to judge?) So which is how I almost wrecked one morning driving to work! A brown bunny runs out in front of me, and I slam on my breaks, almost having the car behind me rear end me, whose driver also worked there. We get to the jobsite, where much screaming and yelling occurred! Then I tell this man a Reader's Digest condensed version of the nun and the brown bunny story. I felt like a prostitute, betraying someone's most dark and intimate secrets, but what choice did I have? Suddenly, this man gets really quiet and calmly says, "Jesus Christ, that's really fucked up, Vaness! I'm sorry!" and just wonders off. Thanks Sister Anita!

<u>The two creepy, but super overly nice people who still to this day, I suspect of being swingers.</u> Now, much like the gay couple that we worked for, I really don't care what anyone's extracurricular hobbies are, as long as they don't involve acts of drowning sacks of kittens or kicking puppies

in the face. This married woman calls one day and asks for an estimate for chain link fence for a dog run. I tell her that sometimes the smaller jobs were more costly due to the amount of travel entailed and smaller amount of work to be done. She says in a breathy voice much to rival that of Jessica Rabbit's, "Well, then, I guess I'm just going to have to put out." Confused, and thinking she had mistakenly said, "pull trout," I asked her to reiterate. Apparently, "put out" was what she DEFINITLY said! I was laughing so bad, that I told her that if she did, I would knock a hundred dollars off of her bill! (Which I actually did.) Now, we go and do this job and during it, this older couple would parade around scantily clad, and offer us lemonade. Much like sensing the reverberations of the Jim Jones Jonestown festival, I always politely declined. I like my roofies in a good martini, for Christ Sakes! Anyways, Bob asks me if I was happening to sense any weird vibrations there. I had to agree! If there was some kind of level beyond weird, it could definitely be defined as this situation! These people were nice and paid on time, though, (thank God that I didn't have to go and retrieve the payment check out of anyone's pants!) We escaped, and, thankfully, SHE was STILL the only one to have to put out!

The poor woman who got screwed. I feel bad when people get taken advantage by contractors. It gives us all bad names. I got a call from a woman who said that one had tried to install a fence for her, failed miserably, and then escaped with her deposit. Sure, we would fix it for her! Upon arrival, it was clear that he didn't know his ass from a hole in the ground, which were quite a misplaced few! This was almost like a scene from Caddyshack if the gopher had been turned loose on Angel Dust! Now, if you've ever tried to install a fence, here's a little rule of advice. I don't care if you have a degree in Quantum Physics, maybe you can explain wormholes in outer space, BUT YOU CANNOT, AND I EXTEMELY EXPRESS CANNOT, DIG YOUR HOLES AHEAD OF TIME, REGARDLESS OF ANY UNBELIEVALE MATHMATICAL SKILLS THAT YOU MAY POSESS! We have tried that avenue, and trust me, it just doesn't work out! Well, if you are unfamiliar with Screamtown, PA, lots have strange lay outs. The houses will be obviously be on the main roads, but the garages will always be located behind them on a back alleyway, forcing the driver to walk down a staircase and through the backyard, to their much cherished homestead. Work ensues for us. One day, installing at the back staircase, I tell Bob that I smell a skunk. He says that there is a college nearby and many dumpsters around, maybe one sprayed the night before. We keep working, when, to me, this stench becomes climactically worse.

I tell him once again, and he, being heavy smoker, much like the operator from Rigatonis who no longer had any olfactory sense in his nostrils, tells me to shut up and keep digging. I happened to pick up my head up and see the worst possible Construction Manger ever imagined! That skunk was sitting there on the steps, about two feet away from my face, watching us working! My body was busy moving, before my mind could completely register the horror before me! Now, Bob, startled by my untimely exit, also looks up, and sees it! Then he takes off running! The skunk, equally startled, comes hauling ass down the staircase after us! Now the whole idea behind having a fence is great. It will hopefully keep vermin out, but if one manages to invade, then sometimes they become irretrievably trapped as well! All three of us were flailing through this yard, like a scene from Benny Hill, but much lacking the nudity or any humor! The skunk was chasing Bob, Bob was chasing me, and in turn, I was chasing the skunk! (I swear to God, I am not making this up!) What the hell was the spray trajectory rating on these critters anyway?!? Thankfully, this particular creature's tank must have been on Empty from the last night's performances! Finally, it found a portion of fence that was not yet installed, and managed to escape, leaving us stinkily unscathed!

A couple from Wilkes Barre that wanted a fence put in their yard for their dogs. This was the best love story EVER told! (Said couple, if you think I am trying to capitalize on your story, you may be partially right or partially wrong. However, I believe that there is so much misery in the world, people need to hear this epic tale of romance!) This couple were very young, with two of the step children being his. The missus was a nurse, and the husband was confined to a motorized wheel chair. She would leave for work in the mornings, and he would eventually emerge and creep around back to have a cigarette behind the shed. DON'T TELL MY WIFE OR CHILDREN, he would scream! I told him, that if someone should happen by, to just fling it over to me, and I would say it was mine. This was strangely reminiscent of my high school bathroom days of sneaking smokes, but yet another symbiotic relationship was formed.

He had an unholy hatred for their father, and when upon arrival, would could come zipping out of the house shrieking, "Oh, look, here comes my children's SPERM DONOR!" This actually lead to my fabulous resume addition of equipment operator, alarm clock manager, glorified babysitter, and now, apparently, domestic dispute advisor! Why couldn't I just dig fucking holes?!? Now, I was raised proper by a Polish family, which basically meant always be polite. If someone had a terrible scar or was missing a limb, don't ask questions, BECAUSE YOU WOULD GET A FUCKING BELTING! So when this particular gent asked me one day, if I ever wondered what happened to him, all the electrical wiring managed to overload in my head. Short circuits and fuses blown everywhere. No! Nope! NO!!! Who's hiding around the corner with a 10 gauge 34 inch piece of leather?!? Me, though, being thoroughly confused as to rather being polite or either rude with not wanting to hear his story, and much like a deer in headlights, was incapable of escape! I was trapped!

Suddenly he tossed me a smoke, and a spark of a friendship kindled. (No pun intended, OK, well, maybe just a little). He proceeds to tell his amazing story. Smoke 'em if you got 'em"! So I sit down in the grass and listen to this tale. (Please now add terrible psychologist to my resume. One would which have people diving off of the Freedom Bridge in Sparks Summit). He was dating this girl, and on trying to impress her and her family, makes Thanksgiving dinner one year. He cooks the turkey in one of those cheap, shitty tin trays and it breaks upon exit of the oven, covering him with scalding, hot grease! No one would offer to take him to the hospital, the family and INCLUDING HIS CUNT GIRLFRIEND! Now, I am weeping. So, he drives himself to the hospital, where he meets this nurse that dresses his 3$^{rd}$ degree burns. They fall in LOVE! (Thanks, Cupid, for blindly and randomly shooting your arrows of affection everywhere)! They ended up TOTALLY falling in love, and getting married. Then tragedy occurred. After a few months of marital bliss, he has a stroke, which renders all his super powers basically powerless. But she NEVER left him, and being the good nurse that she was, always took care of him. The ultimate, "For better or worse," clause here, folks, at its finest! Now I am crying so bad that I think lawn sprinklers would probably not be needed in their back yard for the rest of the season! How was my cigarette not extinguished in this deluge?

He did manage to always keep a sense of humor, though. Oneday Bob and I were working on his side yard. He comes scooting out and says, "I love my wife, but sometimes I just can't deal with her and her stupid, fucking parties!" Whereas, much like a spectacular magician, he manages to throw over his blankets, and like the act of releasing doves out of his sleeve, produces three glasses and a shaker. White Russians for all of us! The Big Lebowski would be so proud! I loved this couple!

<u>Reason for Departure:</u> Unsteady work.

# Chapter 10

<u>McBlame's.</u> While contracting, I was working there during the day, basically just for my health insurance, because the pay was terrible. Two college degrees, and I'm throwing cartons of cigarettes into boxes for $11.00 an hour. The first time I applied to this place, I made the mistake of stating my educational background, and was rejected. The next time I applied, I just blatantly lied, and said I had my GED. HIRED INSTANTLY!

This was a neat system, though! The cartons would come down a line to get a state stamp tax on the bottoms, and then fly through multiple lines, much like resembling a bowling alley, for us to pack in multiple boxes, depending on where they were going to be shipped to. Now, here is the really cool part. There were giant television screens showing the different lanes these cartons would come sailing down in full color and animation. So, this procedure was a little like off track betting, but probably without the repercussions of losing your family's paycheck. But taking into consideration that none of us were making hardly making any money anyway, I guess it would be safe to assume that there wouldn't be much to lose! Aside from that, they did have one good policy. Everyone in upper management had to take turns in performing every job in every department. Such a grand idea! Someone in business management had definitely earned their college degree here, in my humble opinion!

The downfall was, that every morning, probably for insurance reasons, calisthenics had to be done. Now, what with having the contractor's experience, I was no stranger to exercise, so that wasn't the issue. I could toss an 80 pound bag of concrete on my shoulder and motor around with it flawlessly. The problem was, though, was that all of us would have to stand in a circle, much resembling a demented scene from Fight Club. One person was appointed to lead that morning's exercises, whereas the following morning, that person would, in turn, have to select the next day's victim. With only a finger point, some poor bastard would have to lead that day's degrading routine. This act lead to much animosity between employees! Usually, why did you give the finger in life means the bird, but this form of insult was much, MUCH WORSE! Suffering from social anxiety, made this act of torture completely intolerable for me! WHY CAN'T I JUST PUNCH IN AND PACK MY BOXES?!? WHY WAS I BEING FORCED TO LEAD SEMINARS ON FUCKING PHYSICAL TRAINING?!?

Now, this is where the downward spiral of my career there occurred. We had lockers, and were not permitted to keep our excess clothing in the packing areas. On one particular hot morning, I take my sweatshirt off, and it being two hours until break, toss it into one of the boxes. Seemingly thinking it would go unnoticed, I get reprimanded by one of the managers. You'd swear I got caught shooting heroin in the bathroom! It took me awhile, but I finally located the snitch. When confronted, he tries to defend himself by declaring, "Well, I'm going places in this company!" Which I managed to retort in full blown rage disorder, "TRUST ME, YOU LITTLE SHITHEAD, NO ONE IS EVER GOING ANYPLACE, ANYWHERE, AT ANYTIME, IN THIS FUCKING DUMP! EVER! FUCK YOU!" This rant had a terrifying effect on someone who obviously who was not used to confrontation. Nothing was even said to HR! Clearly, he was not of the upper echelon of management material that he thought he was cut out for!

The biggest offender turned out to be the president! That company was presently looking for job bids for snow removal, so I politely approach him and asked if I could perhaps submit one. He looks at me, (and to his credit, probably thinking that I was just one more of the brain dead drones employed there), says to me, "Honey, we need people with REAL companies to bid." That fucking condescending Jew bastard! Both rage disorder and tears broke forth from me that day after work! And I don't mean to ever insult upon our Semitic friends, because, I like everyone unconditionally useless you screw me! Did this man even realize that I had about $250,000 worth of plowing equipment more than capable of maintaining that lot?!? And that I also had a million dollar insurance policy, to boot? Why don't you just pull it out of my ass and throw it in my mouth, YOU FUCKING JEW BASTARD!!!

<u>Reason for Departure:</u> The high levels of stupidity and condescending behavior. Also, someone made me cry. Fuck you again, sir!

# Chapter 11

The American Postal System. This is why crisis management was probably adopted and put into play. Maybe if you are a full time employee, with impeccable benefits, this is a fabulous deal, but if you are a part time worker, you are basically used and discarded like a busted rubber. Now, there are two kinds of postal workers, those that are city workers that ride around in the little white, aluminum trucks in a safe route, and THOSE OF US WHO WERE ASSIGNED TO HELLISH RURAL ROUTES DRIVING OUR OWN VEHICHLES! Well, once again being Heaven's whipping boy, I get assigned to the latter. Now, let me tell you how this job proposition started. I was told that I would be paid for three hours a day, regardless if I managed to accomplish my tasks in less time. Being very efficient in my job skills, this sounded like a great opportunity to me! Unfortunately, the system would do their guesstimation timing system in March, when the mail volume was at an all time low. No Christmas cards, no Mother's Day cards, or IRS envelopes to be processed. And here lies the level of mentality of the workers. They would haul ass during this timing system! People, work slower, YOU WILL GET PAID MORE! Clearly the sheet of logic was blank here.

So I, unfortunately, get hired in December. If you are a normal person capable of reasoning, you would have seen this disaster oncoming at an incredible distance. I, however, did not. I accept this job, hoping for some extra money, but much like the promises in failed relationships, and much like that of ghosts gone past, proved to be supernaturally transparent. I was driving my plow truck on this route, mind you. The township would only plow one lane over the mountain that I had to drive over. This meant that if you met an oncoming vehicle, one person would have to back up at least a quarter mile to the nearest driveway! Go township plowing! Salt, cinders, ashes? Two way streets? What? We are out having coffees with the village stripper, WHO IS PROBABLY MORE ADAPT AT PERFORMING THIS JOB WITH HER PLATFORM SHOES ON, THAN YOU INCOMPETET BOOBS! Don't be afraid to throw down a little antiskid! It's not coming out your pockets! But, no! This trail remained treacherous! Oh, fuck all!

One day, I try and pass a Bestest Buy truck, trying to deliver a refrigerator. Well, my truck slides off the road and into a ditch. They pull me out, and I tell them that I would like to send their company a letter of recommendation. Suddenly, terror breaks out, only to rival that of the women accused at the Salem Witch Trials! "WE'LL LOSE OUR JOBS!", they cried! AND THIS IS WHAT IS WRONG WITH THIS COUNTRY, FOLKS! You try and help someone, AND FUCKING GET IN TROUBLE FOR IT! You're better off being a heartless bastard!

Anyway, my route sucked, also involving things like, GETTING HIRED IN DECEMBER! Packages, PACKAGES EVERYWHERE! Now, unlike people who live in the city, people who live in the country live there because they basically hate everyone or are just social recluses, like myself. Regardless, these select few own large tracts of land WITH EQUALLY LARGE DRIVEWAYS THAT ARE USUALLY ILL MAINTAINED DURING THE WINTER SEASON! So this meant trying to navigate these, to try and deliver a package to a customer that was not home anyway! What, people work during the day?!? Since when did this occur?!? After waiting 5 minutes when fruitlessly ringing the doorbell, this would usually be followed by being chased by one of their (and much like their driveways), ill maintained mutts! Since when did hound dogs become aggressive?!? This transpired to turn a three hour shift into an eight hour day, WHICH I WAS NOT GETTING PAID FOR!!! FUCK THIS SHIT!

Reason for Departure: Because I was basically getting screwed, and not in a good way either! I run into one of the full time carriers one day at Roam Depot, and she starts screeching at me that she got stuck with this route. SUCKS TO BE YOU, BITCH!!! FUCK, YOU,TOO!!!

Reason for Departure: Also, emotional torture!

# Chapter 12

<u>The next stop on my travesty of destruction will go unnamed even on my laptop, due to possible pending lawsuits that could be involved.</u> Once again, I end up working for three brothers. (Does anyone see a pattern here, folks?) Anything involving three brothers will apparently involve epic devastation! Anyway, the amount of weird shit that went on there was absolutely phenomenally indescribable! The owner was a Greek who took me down to his house near the quarry on the day of my hiring. (I should have sensed impending doom immediately, but clearly, I am just stupid. Seriously, I was born REALLY premature, and although possessing spectacular intellectual skills, anything involving upper management or just social skills in general confused me!) Anyway, I sit politely for him to give me my paperwork. (That should have been the first the first warning sign, but being as dense as I am, I didn't think much of it!) Then, as I go to leave, he congratulates on my hiring and kisses my cheek! Jesus, these Greeks sure are friendly! (Oh, my God! Does this seem supremely weird to anyone else?!?) Who cares, I just needed a job!

The mechanic that worked there was incredibly intelligent, though, and had the most supernaturally talented gift for fixing the crappy machinery that was unbelievably used. Did the front end need to be ripped off a loader to just replace one tiny O-Ring? Well, this was your man! Unfortunately, his impeccable intelligence was much rivaled by his short temper! (Which was understanding so, considering the fact that most of these dinosaurs that he was trying to fix, were like trying to make a silk purse out of a pig's ear!) Having to deal with no heat in the garage, and nothing but generators spewing exhaust to run the lighting, made him certifiably crazy. On occasion, and much like a character from a John Irving novel, would load up a rag full of starting fluid, and with the perfected statement of any dictator, would scream indignantly, "I CAN'T TAKE THIS FUCKING PLACE ANYMORE!" and huff the rag, knocking himself out, rendering himself unconscious on the floor! CPR certifications anyone?!?

Now, here is where his little habit almost saved his life! It must have inadvertently managed to kill off every germ or bacteria strain in his system! He would work in a terrible environment and go visit "The Green Office" (the shitter) and come back eating a sandwich! AND HE NEVER GOT SICK! Even I have a high tolerance for grossness, but this was even weird for me! Apparently, he was living in his own little ecosystem of filth, and somehow his body managed to adapt to it! Until one week, he visits his mom down in Florida. Nice weather, a clean condo, and unlimited air conditioning! Well, he returns to work with Strep Throat, and has to stay in the hospital for two days because he can't even swallow or breathe! Stay filthy, people! AND SCREW HAND SANITIZERS!

One day I wander over to his garage, and he asks me if I want to see something cool. He was going to put a loader tire back on its rim. He gets a can of starting fluid out, sprays a line of it across the parking lot, and then fills the rim with it. (Now, if you're a guy, you'll know what he was doing, but I was clueless at the time.) Then he throws me inside the garage, gets out a lighter, and proceeds to light this little pyrotechnic trail up. It looked either like something from a futuristic movie or from a bad Road Runner cartoon, I'm not really sure which! The flames go racing along the sand, and into the tire! KABOOM! And this tire, the size of a spaceship, completely and perfectly launches itself onto the rim! HOLY SHIT! DID I JUST SEE THAT?!? Maybe his abilities involving starting fluid far surpassed that of just inhalation!

His wife was incredibly understanding, though. One day, sitting through a particularly painful 8 hour MSHA class, he nods at me. Lunch break. Oh, LIQUID LUNCH! We go flying along to the local establishment for a 6 pack. Now, on the way back, we're trying to slam these. Being on a dirt road, I don't know what was more shook up, my stomach or the beer! Being a resourceful gent, the mechanic screams, "IF YOU HAVE TO PUKE, AT LEAST ROLL THE WINDOW DOWN!" Then his wife calls. One would think that this would lead to an argument, but apparently the secret to a long marriage is complete honesty. Or a completely complacent wife, at this particular venture, I'm not sure. "Honey," he says, "I can't really talk right now. I got stuck sitting through this torturous meeting, and Ness and I are trying to down this six pack on our lunch break before we get back! Love you!" In which she laughingly let him go! That's 30 years of trust for you! Now, we get back without enough time to consume the last two, so I did the only plausible thing possible…I put them in the quarry's superintendent's truck! Whereas I crept back into the meeting and proceeded to whisper in his ear to make an excuse to leave. Catering was onsite, and cold cuts were available! I have never seen more gratitude expressed in a human being's eyes before!

One day, though, horror was ensued by the mechanic. Our biggest loader only had enough clearance to back into the garage with about roughly an eyelash of room because of the door. Well, he goes to back it in, and apparently the door had rolled down a bit. BOOM! Driven by utter hysterics, the poor mechanic, which had repeatedly proved his competency in fixing garbage, shit there, became completely unglued. All the rest of us stopped what we were doing, and started banging out the dent, once we eventually got the door down! Think teamwork, people!

This was to not be paralleled with my almost, unadmitable disaster. One winter, the lady who ran everything, had to get neck surgery, so I took over her job in the office. We had a couple of laptops there for extraneous things, but there was only one that actually ran everything. The one IN the main office. I'm talking it was THE MASS MOTHERBOARD.

It ran the scale house, the accounting linked on to it, payroll, you name it! So when I crashed it, I was horrified! We were super dead at that time of year, which meant vast amounts of time dedicated to large amounts of depravity! Some days, we were lucky enough to see one elusive truck in an eight hour shift! This made for bored employees to try and create their own fun! The superintendent and I, in a desperate attempt to mentally stimulate ourselves, got into a contest, WHO COULD FIND THE WEIRDEST PORN IMAGINABLE! Now, this contest couldn't involve anything sexy; it had to just be retarded. "I found something with ponies!" I would scream in delight! The superintendent would then retort, "Ya, well I found something involving golf balls and vegetables! So, FUCK YOU!" This evil little game went on for weeks, until the unthinkable happened! I go to scale out a truck full of antiskid, and the computer locks up on me with the added insult of a Viagra ad stuck on the screen!

Thankfully, the driver at the window had a sense of humor! FUCK THINK, VANESS! I'm not very technologically savvy, but I tried everything possible. Shut the computer off and try rebooting it, much to no avail! Try logging on under someone else's name. NOTHING! FUCK!!! The supervisor, being equally as inadequate as myself in this field, was completely useless in solving this matter! FUCK, AGAIN!!! So for days I was stuck handwriting tickets out, which I didn't mind, but eventually this shit was going to have to be electronically entered in for billing purposes. My prayers were answered when a DOT official showed up. These people are usually looking for a place to hide during the winter time, but this guy actually took mercy upon my soul. It took him 7 hours to unlock this beast. Antiviruses were downloaded, hair was ruffled, but he eventually ACCOMPISHED THE TASK! What could I possibly offer this stoic man in terms of reward? A free lunch, car detailing, a hand job? He declined all of my offers, saying it was just in the interests of helping a fellow employee! What a guy!

This leads to the story of Potato Rock. Now, things in life were absolutely terrible for some of us. Both the quarry superintendent and I were about to lose our houses, which we had worked so hard over the years to earn. We were probably both as equally suicidal, and I'm not joking, either. One day, we are driving through excavation, when I see this little screened rock in the middle of the road. "STOP THE GOD DAMN TRUCK, I NEED THAT!!!" I scream! I know most women crave diamonds and fancy dinners, BUT I NEEDED THIS STUPID FUCKING ROCK! I grab it, and take it back to the lab. This is where Potato became a legend! (This is because it indeed, truly looked like a Potato!) In efforts cheer each other up, we would take turns, and hide it in all strange places! The refrigerator, a filing cabinet, the glove compartment! Potato was lurking everywhere! Suddenly, this extraneous piece became more powerful than any antidepressant ever produced on the market! Where would it turn up next?!? In the microwave, the coffee maker, the toilet tank like the Beatles' Yellow Submarine? Who knew!!! This rock possessed unbelievable powers to induce incredible happiness! In what lunch box would it be found in today?!? Eventually, it came to reside on my desk in the lab room in a nest I made for it. When questioned by DOT, I became vehemently irate! THAT'S A SPECIAL SAMPLE!

Well, it's been 12 years, and you know what? I STILL HAVE FUCKING POTATO! I take it on every major jobsite with me! One day, a DOT official calls me about something, and then jokingly asks if I still have Potato. I immediately send him a text with a picture on it of it being on my dashboard of my company truck. Once again, Potato never failed to make someone laugh! What secret mineral was in this particular specimen, anyway? Magical properties installed by some elemental mage? What?!?

This leads to the owner, which pretty much made the rest of us look like saints...by far, in any comparison. Much like Scotty, he was an absolute wonder to the human ability to imbibe uncontrollably and survive (and, probably to the wonder of eventual forensic scientists everywhere) how he not only managed to compose himself on a daily basis, but to ALSO TO NOT MANAGE TO OVERDOSE SIMULTANEOUSLY! Much like Mr. Crab, he was prone to extreme emotional outbursts! The only redeeming value, was that he had hazel eyes. Now, this is weird, but I never could bring myself to trust someone with brown eyes... because THEY ARE ALWAYS FUCKING BROWN! But it's easy to gauge someone's disposition with light eyes. Green, blue, hazel, look for pupil dilation! But this man's hazel eyes changed color with the indication of a traffic control light! Blue meant he was in a good mood, green meant that he could be moderately tolerated, and muddy brown was a terrible harbinger signal for his indescribable rage disorder. Not only was I well versed at gradations involving aggregate, but I also now possessed the capabilities of a crystal ball reading, telepathy, with optometrist skills in the mix! Was there a special certification offered for this particular gift?!? NO! Just keep getting those samples and running those shakers, Vaness!

At the same time, I was bartending at the Stonehouse on the weekends, which I deemed the Stoner House, BECAUSE EVERONE THERE KEPT TIPPING ME IN POT! I'm no angel when it comes to illegal pharmaceutical usage, but the one thing I absolutely will not do is smoke reefer. It makes me extremely paranoid and cry uncontrollably for hours, regardless of the strain! So there I found myself, always having a purseful of it! PEOPLE, I WANT MONETARY CASH! I CANNOT MAKE MY TRUCK PAYMENT IN WEED! The banks don't value that kind of currency! So I improvise. One day I'm dropping off paperwork over the quarry owner's house, and he starts bitching about the fact that no one but the mechanic gave him a Christmas present. I just thought he wanted to be left alone. What could I possibly give to the man who had everything? Then I improvised! I regifted! I put my impressive stash into a box, with a warning label on it, much to rival that of accidental ingestion of antifreeze to house pets. Usually, threats would read, "Do not open until Christmas!" Mine read, "UNDER ABSOLUTELY NO CIRCUMSTANCES, WHATSOEVER, DO NOT FUCKING OPEN THIS PACKAGE IN THE PRESENCE OF OTHERS!" So I give it to him in my lab room. He was parked outside my window, and only with the glee to surpass that of a small child on a holiday morning, rips into this illicit gift…and then just sits there, motionless, with his head down. Now, I have a problem in life; it's the terrible habit of wreckless spontaneity. "WHAT HAVE I FUCKING DONE? WHO GIVES THEIR BOSS CANNABIS AS A BELATED CHRISTMAS GIFT?!?" I actually was getting ready to start cleaning out my desk, (come on Potato, gather your belongings, too!) when he comes flying in the room, and gives me the biggest bear hug ever! Most of the time you lose a job for doing drugs, but apparently, this was reverse psychology! You were rewarded for it!

Ours was a love/hate relationship. Much like Pat, he had a nice side where he gave me my training for free, but those kaleidoscope eyes were wrecking it, depending on how much skiing the Snowman did. On one particular day, when the optical department much resembled a mud puddle, we got into a spectacular fight about billing that seriously almost turned into a fist fight. I'M NOT KIDDING, EITHER! Our biggest client threatened to drop us! Tempers flared and left aftermath much like the damage done after a detonation of a hydrogen bomb! The owner goes home that night not to his house next to the quarry, but in another state in a rage after finally admitting that this issue was not my fault. Sore loser! The next day he returns at roughly the early afternoon, and starts repeatedly calling my cell, whereas I REPEATLY IGNORED HIM! The kiss ass overachiever scalehouse lady comes racing into the lab room and hyperventilates that the owner was trying to get a hold of me. I tell her, "I know. I'm well aware of that. I'm just fucking ignoring him." She was truly horrified by this admission! If you want Pavlov's dogs, try looking someplace else! The only occupant of this room was the technician!

Fine, I call him, and he is beside himself! "Come down here with a tape measure!" he screams! So, I grab one from the garage mechanic, (that's unusually coherent), and go ripping down to the house. COPS EVERYWHERE! EVERYWHERE! WAS THERE A MURDER INVOLVED?!? I prayed that no bodies were to be found! However, there's a lot of room to hide a body in a 400 acre place! What did I need a tape measure for?!? Coffin sizes?!? Now my aversion to these people in blue was much like that to vampires to sunlight! Utter paranoia ensued upon arrival. What had I to cover up for?!? What excuses were to be made?!? What the hell was illegal in my truck?!? Why am I such a shitty liar?!? Focus, FOCUS! FUCK!!! OK, Vaness, try and operate under some kind of façade of normalcy! I enter to the witness intense questioning of the defendant, which was clearly robbed. Having being asked if he had perhaps any disputations lately, he denies it, waits for connotations to be made, and then manages to rabbit punch me in the back of the neck when no one was looking. FUCK! This wasn't in my job description! The entourage makes their great egress, and the man wants me to measure and install a new door for him!

I didn't have the heart to tell him that he probably let THE WRONG ONE IN! So, I go and get my measurements. Now, there was roughly about twenty other workers employed at this quarry at this time that were males. WHY WAS I STUCK WITH CONDUCTING THIS HELLACIOUS

PROJECT?!? He tells me to pick a slab door to replace the damage, and I argue with him that usually exterior doors come with frames. Now he's just pissing me off! The situation that initially started out with my sympathy, turned into shrieking! "Fine, just take the company card and go!" he yells. "WELL, IS IT ACTUALLY GOING TO WORK FOR ONCE?!?" I screamed back!

Then I set off on my epic journey to Blowe's with a company truck with a cracked frame, and a credit card of questionable legality. I return unscathed from my adventure to try and install it, only to argue with the owner (ONCE AGAIN, but really, what else was ever new around there?). I was just trying to install the door as directed! I had all the tools ready and had multiple experiences in placing them, even in older houses that were no longer plumb or level. "No, I will do it!" He shouts. "You can't even tie your own shoes!" I ballisticly erupt! He then proceeds to rip the brand new door out of the frame, and throws it where the old one should have been replaced. Now, I can deal with a lot in life, but the one thing I CANNOT TOLERATE IS SHITTY CRAFTMANSHIP! It was like watching a girl get an abortion with a rusty tin can or a broken Coke bottle! (My, apologizes, Virginia Rappe!) What the hell?!?

Now, one morning, his wife calls from a different state in complete terror! Her husband wasn't answering his calls for hours! She is completely hysterical, much like portraying the innocence of a young girl with a lost kitten, and overly apologetic. I felt terrible both for her, being that fucking, stupidly naive, and for him, wondering if he had accidentally overdosed and had been ransacked by yet another hooker! So I did the only thing possible in my powers of reasoning, I FUCKING LIED! I said that maybe he was out on the crusher and couldn't hear his phone ring. Trying to buy time, I said that I would call her back. Well, I CB out there, much to no avail! No owner to be found anywhere! GOD DAMN IT! NOW I'M A NERVOUS WRECK! GREAT! MORE COPS! MORE EXCUSES TO BE MADE! THERE IS ONLY A CERTAIN DEGREE OF LEVEL FOR COVERING THAT YOU CAN DO FOR ONE PERSON! Where was he? Did we keep adrenaline syringes in our medicine cabinet?!? Oh, no! They were supposed to be refrigerated anyway! Was there any tools in our shop capable of removing wire ties, 12 gauge rope, or police issued handcuffs maintained enough without the threat of high voltage shock? Think Vaness, THINK!!! (On second hand, I was under the impression that on occasion, much like Frankenstein, sometimes high voltage lead to resurrection!) We certainly had quite a collection of hardware with frayed cords!

Now the other office lady and I flip a quarter to see who was going to be the victim of having to go down to his house, and probably WITNESS THE CARNAGE! (Or possibly the unbridled humor unleashed, depending on your perspective!) I lose, and thankfully he calls! "What the hell was the problem?" "YES, WHAT WAS THE PROBLEM, INDEED!?! I THOUGHT YOU WERE DEAD DOWN THERE BY AN O.D. AND PROVOKED HEART ATTACK BROUGHT ON BY OVEREXERTION BY SOME UKRANIAN PROSTITE WITH A CARROT

UP YOUR ASS, YOU JERKOFF!!! CALL YOUR WIFE! SHE'S FUCKING HYSTERICAL!!!" I scream! "I was on a conference call," he says. I calm down by now and say to him, "I'll give you ten minutes to CALL ME BACK WITH A BETTER FUCKING EXCUSE!" Then I slam down the phone! Now, the self righteous, other office lady is horrified! "I can't believe you just said that to him!" And having slowly amassed the same amount of hatred and apathy as the garage mechanic, I shriek at her! "I DON'T CARE ANYMORE, YOU CONDESCENDING, CUNT! FUCK YOU, TOO!" Thank God for not having any HR Department!

Then he shows up in the office later and says to me, "I just want you to know, that there are no errant vegetables in any orifices of my body anywhere!" (Boy, that was something to be proud of!) I stare at him and then say, "Are you sure? Because I'm on the clock, and could check for you in case that you are mistaken!" "Why do you always have to be such an asshole, Vaness?!?" was screamed! "Why do I always cover for you, you irresponsible dick?!?" I scream back! Now the office bitch is really upset and starts yelling for us to calm down! We both scream in unison, "WILL YOU JUST SHUT THE HELL UP ALREADY?!?" Then we both walk out, leaving her to ponder her uselessness in ending this epic tirade! She might have been good at her job, but she was absolutely terrible at resolving manager/employee relations!

<u>Honorable Mentions for the Coolest People that I have ever met.</u> The lowboy driver. His job entailed hauling our shitty equipment to different states, depending on where jobsites were located. He comes in my lab room one day and tells

me a story. Now, common sense, when you haul equipment, it's best to do it at night or in the wee hours of the morning, when traffic is the lightest. So, he gets to the quarry at 4 A.M. and can't find the dozer. He calls one of the brothers and is cryptically told to "Walk the land!" CLICK! He starts screaming, "Walk the land?!? What am I, A FUCKING INDIAN? I'm just some guy from Jersey! There's 400 acres here, and it's pitch black! There's shit out here in PA that will fucking kill you...wolves, snakes, probably assorted turtle species out there that had capabilities of contracting rabies, thus rendering them with supernatural rage disorder powers! WALK THE FUCKING LAND?!? FUCK YOU!!! I have a wife and kids! I am not going to leave them homeless and indigent because of your state's unmanageable wildlife!" At this point in time, I thought I should bring it to his attention that New Jersey was well known and much loathed for its incredible tick population! I felt equal reservations about traveling there, as well! But I did not ruin this impressive rant with my stupid interjections!

<u>Honorable Mentions for, well you know what, I just can't label anything anymore. Who cares at this point?!?</u> One afternoon, I'm running the scalehouse, and the phone rings. It's the new quarry superintendent from Jersey. "TWOMMY'S TRUWCK IS ON FIWORE!" he shrieks! Now, I start reprimanding him, saying that although we always joked around there, certain shit was just not deemed funny! Well, this was no joke! Tommy's truck was suddenly engulfed in flaming lava like the final scene from the original Wicker Man movie! (But without the livestock sacrificed, or Tommy, either, thankfully for that matter! I don't have a

clue what the Gods would have traded us for him anyway! Perhaps some magical beans or a ball of twine?) Probably if I threw in that worthless superintendent, we could have gotten some shiny tin foil! So I quickly call 911! SEND HELP! What hell? The quarry superintendent was suddenly incapable of dialing three numbers? I wasn't being lazy, I WAS TRYING TO SAVE PRECIOUS TIME!!!

The fire truck shows up, and not being familiar with our surroundings, was completely at a loss as to where to go. Suddenly, I was inexplicably possessed by the giggles! (Now, this actually isn't funny, because this driver of the haul truck could have perished, but I've read literature stating that some people's coping mechanisms during times during times of epic disaster, just cause their minds to completely malfunction!) "JUST WALK THE LAND!", I wanted to scream! "JUST WALK THE FUCKING LAND, ALREADY!" Instead, I told them to go up the crusher side AND LOOK FOR THE FUCKING SMOKE! By the time the inferno was extinguished, there was absolutely nothing left to this wreck, but a flaming skeleton. Thankfully, aside from the truck's untimely demise, at least both Tommy's skeleton, epidermis, and respiratory system were viable! Thanks, God, and inadequate quarry superintendents everywhere!

I would, however, manage to torture the owner in countless ways in retaliation for his extreme insolence. I once wrote him a 4 page manifesto on the "Top Ten Reasons Why I Thought He Sucked," complete with explicit and definitive reasons why I thought he was a dick. I stapled it to his desk.

Once again, thinking that this ill thought out action on my part would require immediate relocation, I started cleaning out my desk. (Boy, the amount of crap that you manage to amass!) Come on, Potato, we're out of here! You ride shot gun! Instead, he comes in my lab room, dying laughing! It was completely impossible to gauge this man's emotions! It was definitely a blue eyed day, thankfully!

Another time, knowing that he had a meeting planned in his office, my deviant behavior resubmerged. Now, our offices were actually classy, being two trailers pinned together, but due to poor foundations, if you put enough weight in any given room, would cause the flimsy doors to shut. So I snuck into his office and tacked a poster on the back of his door. In the middle of the meeting, as surmised, the door swings shut to reveal the absolutest porn thought imaginable! "WHAT THE FUCK, VANESS!" was screamed! "HOW COME EVERYTIME SOMETHING HAPPENS AROUND HERE, IT'S ALWAYS MY FUCKING FAULT?!?" I yell back!

We also had huge job bid boards that were the white erasable kind that you could use markers on. So I would wipe off all the pertinent information, and just basically draw quarry related murals on them, much to the horror of the office bitch. The owner loved them, though, which only added to her seething hatred and resentment for me. He definitely had an eye for art, no matter what color the eyes on that particular day!

He also had the creepy habit of asking me to drop paperwork off at his house WHEN HE WAS STILL IN BED! (I'm not even sure if he was completely naked or not!) One day, I particularly lost my temper and go over there, and toss a whole bunch of files all over his room! "I HAVE TO DRIVE AN HOUR AND A HALF TO WORK EVERYDAY AND THEN AGAIN BACK HOME, AND YOU'RE STILL IN BED! YOU PICK THIS SHIT UP!" I scream! "What the hell is wrong with you?!?" he screams back! "YOU!" I shout back!

Well, I got back at him! One day, I am once again summoned to bring paperwork to his house. He goes into the bathroom for an extended break, and when he finally returns, I say the most awesomest thing ever! "I have hidden my panties somewhere in this place! They might be in your pillow case, under your couch cushions, or in your refrigerator's fruit drawer." He shrieks, "GOD DAMN IT, VANESS! WHAT IF MY WIFE SHOWS UP?!?" "Too bad!' I retort. "Happy hunting!" I yell, as I march out through the door, leaving him in absolute terror, to spend the rest of the day ripping his house apart, fruitlessly searching for a pair of nonexistent undergarments! At least he didn't make it back to the quarry that day to relentlessly irritate me like usual!

The funniest thing that ever happened was when the owner accidentally saw my purse open in the office. Most women carry tissues, lipgloss, stupid receipts, what have you. Well, I had a 9 MM in mine! He, being from out of state, was clearly not versed in mine's ability to issue pistol permits! "WHAT THE FUCK, VANESS! THERE'S A GUN IN YOUR FUCKING PURSE!" he screams! "WHAT THE FUCK ARE YOU DOING GOING THROUGH MY

PURSE, ANYWAY, YOU ASSHOLE?!?" I yell! "I HAVE TO CLOSE UP THE BAR AT NIGHT. DO YOU THINK I'M GOING TO WALK OUT TO MY CAR ALONE AND UNARMED?!?" Now, having a plethora of daughters, ironic to the construction trade, he looks at me quietly for a full minute and finally says, "Well, ya, I guess that's a good idea." Which is how I ended up shooting with him! I'm leaving work, and he calls me. "I've got a friend over here. Bring your arms!"

Now, I have a steadfast, loyal logic where I won't touch a gun when I've been drinking, so I stop by, and we are having a good time. I let the quarry owner repeatedly shoot my gun, and then decided to screw with him. "NOW YOU ARE DONE FOR!" "Why?," he inquires. "Because I'm going to take that gun and shoot my worst exboyfriend with it, and your fingerprints are all over it!" "YOU, SICK, TWISTED, FUCK!" he screams! (Oh, such compliments, ladies! Screw that, you look pretty in that outfit, crap!) His friend was laughing so hard, he didn't have to worry about death by a ricochet! I thought he should be more concerned about an internal rupture!

Years later, on a whim, I decided to go and visit this quarry owner unexpectedly, and equally unexpectedly, he was delighted to see me! He gives me a hug and a big kiss on the side of the head, and then offers to have a beer with me. So having a short attention span, I go wandering around his living room, randomly poking at things. I happened to pick up a book off of his coffee table, when a condom comes flying out of it and lands on the floor! (These, Greeks, still so friendly after all these years!) Then I start screaming at him! "You, idiot! What if your wife found this?!? And you probably didn't even read this book, you just leave it on your table so the ladies think that you are an intellect!" (Which in all sincerity, I actually had to look up what this tome was about.) After hearing his imbecilic response for an excuse, I scream, "Nothing has changed over all this time!!! I don't even work here anymore! I can't babysit you forever!" And once again, I marched out through his door! Thanks for the beverage!

<u>Reason for departure:</u> At this point in time, the list was longer than both of my shirt sleeves put together! When I gave my notice, I shook hands with the owner, and he said the weirdest thing, "I truly and most sincerely wish you the best of luck…but you'll never make it there. You are too smart and creative, and this new company will manage to crush any piece of individuality remaining in your head, TO ABSOLUTELY FUCKING NOTHING!" Then he commenced weeping and left. Jesus, was he ever right!

# Chapter 13

<u>Pack and Shove Supply.</u> This was a blacktop plant. I never had any prior experience, but this place was willing to train and offered reprieve from Quarry Madness! This company was in a big hurry to install this plant in a desolate place with the hopes of increasing their profits by the repairing the destruction of the roads caused by the gas drilling in my area. What seemingly was a plausible idea at the time on their part, turned out to be a lesson in complete and total financial devastation! First, when buying quarries, and trying to sell their wares to DOT, perhaps someone should, I don't know, PERHAPS KICK THE FUCKING IDEA AROUND OF SAMPLING THE STONE BEFORE THE INVERSTMENT IS MADE?!? SEND IT OFF TO SOME LAB, NO MATTER HOW GOD DAMN INADEQUATE IT'S RESULTS USUALLY REGISTER?!? Because this quarry's stone couldn't even compare to the aggregate I used to dump on the garbage in the landfill! Yes! Crappy product coming to a roadway in PA anywhere! Secondly, they were in such a mad hurry to install this plant, my lab room was a shipping container. It was stuck out in the open without insulation. If you are unfamiliar with the asphalt industry, there are many stoves and ovens involved,

which, in the summertime, combined with the direct sun, managed to heat this room to the degree that to rivaling a solar flare! Cocktails, horderves, fire retardant suits anyone? THESE COCKSUCKERS! Thirdly, this is where it took me little time to assess my Quality Control boss was a complete and total blithering idiot. This condemning accusation also encompassed the President and Vice President of that region, in my opinion. On having to take my initial certifications, he comfortingly tells me, "Don't worry if you fail them, I did the first time I took them, too. "WHAT THE HELL KIND OF ADVICE IS THAT TO AN EMPLOYEE?" And furthermore, who gets the job of managing a QC Department and can't even pass the fucking test to be a technician?!? Even I sailed through it with a bit of studying!

So, now the Three Stooges come up with a plan! And much like clowns throwing pies at each other, was about as about effective, if one wasn't considering the comedy factor (or considering the fact that clowns actually have to graduate from an accredited college). Our sand was dirty, they exclaimed! Me, having worked at an aggregate quarry, suggests getting a classifier. (If you are unfamiliar with these devices, they basically just clean sand.) "We've got an idea!" they exclaim again! Let's pay the technicians excessive amounts of overtime to come up with new mix designs using sand from a quarry 70 miles away! WHY THE FUCK WOULD SOMEONE BUY A QUARRY, ERECT AN ASPHALT PLANT, AND THEN HAVE PRODUCT SHIPPED IN?!? Once again, classifier anyone? So, now they pay drivers with their triaxles to only haul in sand! CAN ANYONE JUST BUY A FUCKING CLASSIFIER

AROUND HERE ALREADY?!? These drivers weren't even backhauling anything! This meant it basically cost the company $200,000 of losses instead of a $300,000 investment!

The poor sales kid went bonkers one day and screamed, "I can't take this bullshit anymore! Every time I make a sale, IT ACTUALLY COSTS THIS COMPANY MONEY!!! WHAT THE FUCK ALREADY?!?" So after a premeeting was held for the meeting for the postmeeting, an agreement was come to by upper management! Maybe we should get a classifier! Mother…of…God!

Now, here was the problem: my boss who was clearly inept at his job, had to rely on the guy who worked with me to do it for him. In turn, this guy I worked with, was granted free reign over whatever he felt like doing! He would insist upon doing the first round of testing when it was 5 A.M. and cool. He would then vanish for the rest of the day over to the dispatch room where the air conditioning was running on full bore and the most plushest couch ever manufactured, offered its sensual touch to any ass implanted upon it! This much left me to deal with the raging inferno (probably dealt by Prometheus, himself) of the lab room by myself for the rest of the 16 hour day. What a dick!

Now, three of us get sent up to Alfred University, that specializes in engineering, in New York to get certified for blacktop there. (And you know what, I have used pseudo names for every other place in this book here, but I am still so pissed off, THAT THIS IS THE REAL FRIGGING NAME! FUCK YOU, ALFRED!) Anyway, this was all part of my company's mastermind plan to be able to ship over the border. Well, folks, if our material wasn't passing in PA, it sure as shit wasn't going to pass by New York's strict standards! But, hell, I'm a team player (isn't that obvious by now? SARCASM ALERT! BLARING SIRENS EVERYWHERE!). This was a two day class, followed by a test on the third day. By day one, it was clear that this class was a joke! The material presented was that of the mentality of, "See Jane run. Watch Spot jump!" AND it was an open book test! So the night before the big finale, we all get trashed. Once again, thanks box red wine for another charming hangover! We all miserably suffer through taking the test.

After a few weeks, our results come back to the office. Only Dick passes! WHAT?!? I HAVE NEVER FAILED A TEST IN MY LIFE!!! Now I have to contend with utter confusion, self reprimand, and having to hear Dick repeatedly throw it in my face, "I'M THE ONLY ONE WHO PASSED! I SHOULD GET A RAISE!" Two weeks go by, and I can't take it anymore! So, I call the Alfred office and politely inquire if someone there would be so kind as to possibly go over my answers, and let me know what mistakes I made. "Sure!" I was promised, and much like a first date gone horribly awry, no phone calls were ever returned. Another two weeks of dealing with Jerkoff patting himself on the back, like a peacock sporting his tail feathers! OH, THIS IS TOO MUCH ALREADY! I call their office again, subsequently, not as polite as the original time. "WHAT THE HELL DID I DO WRONG? CAN SOMEONE GET OFF FACEBOOK ALREADY AND JUST FUCKING

HELP ME?!?" I scream! Strangely, my tirade brought me final justice! My call was actually returned with a plethora of apologies! "I'm sorry, but your test was incorrectly scanned!" This was coming from a MAJOR engineering university! What hungover college student had managed to screw my results up?!? God Damn it! How many other people had this happened to? Seriously?!? Only verbal apologies were ever made, no literary ones ever surfaced, but I made my own sweet revenge! I waited until Asshole was in the asphalt tower with all of his cronies, and then made my grand entrance! "I really did pass my test for New York! They just screwed my test results up!" I exclaimed! The look of horror on his face was absolutely priceless! Right in front of everyone! He starts babbling uncontrollably asking questions! Suddenly, this bird was missing tail feathers, and I WAS RESPONSIBLE! The suffering of my part was ALL WORTH IT!

So now winter rolls around, and he asks to get laid off and does. I also asked for a lay off, but am told NO! by my idiot boss. This response was asinine for two reasons. Number 1 was that once you have DOT approved piles at your quarry, it really doesn't matter what you make to run through the bins for the blacktop. So as long as the plant doesn't blow a hole in one of the screens that sift the rock, you will in all probability have the same level of conformance of your product. Any good quarry manager or loader operator should be able to spot this problem in a heartbeat! Reason Number 2 was much related to Reason Number 1. If the plant didn't need perfect material, THEN WHY THE HELL WAS I DRIVING TEN HOURS A WEEK TO GET PAID FOR A 40 HOUR WORK WEEK?!? OH, THAT'S IT,

KIDS! EVERYBODY OUT OF THE FUCKING POOL! At this point in time, I was so enraged, that I basically just didn't give a shit anymore! So I put my wasted art education skills to work! We were working with a skeleton crew, so hardly anyone was ever around, supervisors included. Our timesheets were on 8 X 11 pieces of paper that had to be submitted daily (not the kind that you are thinking about… the little manila 4 X 8 ones, that had to usually be submitted weekly.) I systematically went into the office and would just randomly punch into the time clock, just to get samples of the numbers. Then I would go down to my lab room and load them into my computer using the scanner. Every day I would show up an hour late and leave an hour early. I would just basically use Photoshop to print out a fake timecard and toss it on the company's desk! Much like a bank robber, I had to be flawless in my calculations! One mistake, and I would be screwed! No amount of explaining would manage to cover my illicit behavior!

Things were getting out of control on my end! I was supposed to go up on the mountain twice a day to take 5 gallon bucket samples of each of the aggregates (this just basically means stone, to all you people unfamiliar with quarry lingo) produced and bring them to the lab for testing. Out of shear enragement, I would put on a good horse and pony show. I would get my samples, take them down the mountain, where I was unmonitored, AND FLING THEM OFF THE BACK OF TRUCK!!! FUCK THIS SHIT! SERIOUSLY, FUCK THIS SHIT! Then I would go and fudge my numbers of the gradations on the laptop. This lead to endless hours of fuckery on my part.

At first, I had this obsession with these, "Find the Hidden Object," games. So I would spend a vast amount of time downloading these games, and then trying to find a shoe, tweezers, a barrette, or a cricket, whatever! Then I would uninstall the program from the company's computer, just because I was bored that there was no cell service there (Just one more reason I was getting screwed!). Now, driven by overachievement my whole life, I realized that although this was amusing, it was not a very positive venue to pursue. Therefore, I decided to enlighten my horizons! I managed to download and print out a four folder tome of, "How to do your taxes!" Which has helped me to this day! Thanks online help and unregulated supervision any day!

The only redeeming value of this company was although my lab completely sucked, THEY INSTALLED THE BEST BATHROOM EVER! Usually, when you are on a jobsite, you get stuck using Green Offices (and that really sucks if you are a woman, freezing cold in the dark in the morning trying to do certain things), but this thing was ABSOLUTELY SPECTACULAR! It was huge, heated, had walls of concrete, and tiled floors! If ever there was an impending nuclear attack, this is where I was coming with hundreds of cans of soup, water, and a can opener! (Can't forget that last item. That would be awkward!) I was so thankful to have this bathroom, that I would go in there twice a week and clean it. This was an actual easy job because the guys I worked with were actually very well housetrained. I would spray everything with cleaner and then fill 5 gallon buckets up with water, and then just basically throw them everywhere! (Much like my lab samples!) Then the drain in the middle of the floor would suck up all the residual filth! This was actually a delightful reprieve from my labroom torture!

Then oneday, someone manages to defile my sanctuary! This guy shows up running though the parking lot, holding his ass with his hand shouting, "Werew is the batroom?" At first I was confused by this question (wondering where we kept the bat collection. Was there a separate building for them to be housed? Who was supposed to feeding these things anyways? Were they starving? Were they lonely? Did they need individual hugs? I thought we were just an asphalt plant!) but then I suddenly realized from his antics, that I didn't need an interpreter, and he was just urgently looking for the bathroom. He was just from New Jersey! "The big square building behind me," I say and point.

This was a terrible mistake on my part, because I go to use this after he leaves, and discover the giant shit storm left behind! Poo everywhere! On the walls, all over the floor, and unexplainably on the sink! It looked like the ending to some terrible German porn scat video! Now, I don't care what kind of dysentery or gastral intestinal disorders you may have in life, but there were plenty of cleaning supplies available there! Just clean up after yourself! My Porcelain Palace was ruined! I get one of my fellow workers and show him the devastation! He stands there for a full minute, completely speechless. Then he says the most ironic thing, "Holy Shit!" Well, there definitely was a lot of shit in there, but I highly doubt any of it was Holy! "Don't worry, Vaness, for once I will clean the bathroom. You do it all the time!"

And he did, too! How could some people be so thoughtful, and others so gross at the same time?!?

<u>Reason for Departure</u>: The owner of the last company was right. If you've ever seen that Pink Floyd video where all the children are mindlessly programmed to march down that hallway, I think I was trapped in an endless loop of it! Safety meetings here, safety meetings there, safety meetings everywhere! Hey, maybe if you're a company so concerned with it, TRY AND HIRE EMPLOYEES WITH IQ'S IN THE TRIPLE DIGIT RANGE! THAT WOULD PREVENT A LOT OF FUCKING DISASTERS THERE, I WOULD THINK! PROBLEM SOLVED! And when I left, that condescending, bitchy HR woman insisted on paraphrasing my written exit interview! "Vanessa believes that she was unjustly doing the vast majority of the job needed to be performed here." I guess that sounded more eloquent than my original, "I'M SICK AND TIRED OF COVERING FOR THE LAZY FUCK THAT I WORK WITH!!!"

But here is where poetic justice comes into play. Supposedly, these exit interviews were to be given to the president to acknowledge, which anyone would think that they would really be filed under "G" for Garbage. Well, just like fashion trends in Paris change, the reign of the old dominion was replaced by, let's just say more observant and competent individuals, which also have probably far better fashion statements in their repertoire. One day, the new president shows up for a routine check, and finds the guy who used to screw me over, fast asleep on the asphalt dispatch couch,

AND GOES FRIGGING BALLISTIC! Now production was momentarily at a halt to have the loader and excavator having to come down off the top of the mountain to pull this couch out of the upper tower AND FUCKING LIGHT IT ON FIRE! Goodbye sensual cushion maiden, and GOODBYE Pack and Shove Supply!

# Chapter 14

<u>Bastard's' Concrete.</u> This was an initial reprieve from the (literal stinking) asphalt industry. Now, here was the issue. I've always had a problem with face blindness. This is called Prosopagnosia. If you put a gun against my head and asked me to draw a picture of my deceased parents, you might as well as pull the trigger, because I couldn't recall! This was terrible in my bartending days, because I would repeatedly not know customers for years! So then I devised a system! I would remember their voices, the way they walked, and their mannerisms. (This seems like I was being very attentive, but in reality, I was just trying to figure out WHO THE HELL EVERYONE WAS!!!) Well, this sensory deprivation managed to almost destroy my emotional one! For the first half a year, the dispatcher would call down, "Test so and so's truck." Who the hell was this person, and all the trucks were painted exactly the same! I couldn't tell anything apart! This would lead me to screaming out in the parking lot out of complete confusion and fear, "WHOSE FUCKING TRUCK SHOULD I BE TESTING?!?" At first, I'm sure that these guys probably thought I was a complete shrew, but by the later part of the year, they all loved me! Seriously. Trucks would come flying up to the lab door. "Pick me,

coach, put me in the game!" And slowly, I started to learn their faces! This was a complete miracle in itself!

The only other redeeming value of this place, was that on one of the first times I was sent to one of their other plants, I FOUND A SEA OF PORN ON THEIR DESK! This managed to completely horrify the dispatcher in charge! Thinking that I would immediately call HR, "OH, NO!" he cried! "OH, YES!" I CRIED! That dickhead, Mark, at least did not manage to infiltrate this place! Now, men are very strange creatures. They will look at porn by themselves, but if a woman is around, they will become utterly paranoid! I'm not really sure if this phenomenon is brought on by parental upbringing or just jealous housewives and/or crazy girlfriends. It took weeks of me working there, but finally these guys got comfortable around me! I would arrange contests where I would lay out random centerfolds, and make the drivers decide on who had the worst boob jobs! "I think Miss May!" they would exclaim! Or, "I think Miss October, but she's got a great ass!" they would proclaim! "You idiots," I would yell! "This is all air brushed anyways!" (Occasionally, I would get some thoughtful driver, who would actually read some woman's short, brainless autobiography, and then say, "I think it's really nice that she likes unicorns and rainbows!" That's when I would just basically grab one of these magazines and belt him upside the head with it!") Then I would take a running tab on what the results were! This would waste endless hours of company time! These guys eventually came to adore and trust me! What other woman would do this?!?

But this job entailed much physical hardship! These gas companies were running balls to the wall installing compressor stations all year long. They would be pouring 300 yard foundations in January, WHEN IT WAS 4 FUCKING DEGRESS OUT! "We want every truckload tested!" these bastards would demand! Now, there were two things wrong here. First, trucks could carry only 10 yards each, so this meant testing 30 trucks in a row! Nonstop! Red and whites flying in everywhere! I'm working under the pressure to rival any air traffic controller! Secondly, every time that you do a test, you have to wash out your equipment, air meters, slump cones, etc. This was an awesome feat to be performed in such frigid temperatures! (Can't I just train tigers, anyone? It would probably less detrimental to my health!) When you use this equipment, you can't wear gloves, because you need your dexterity. I'm covered in water from trying to wash this shit and slowly dying of hypothermia! And so was my equipment! I'd have to hold it behind the truck's exhaust just to make sure it still worked! At this point in time, I'm jealous, because I wanted to be the one behind the truck's exhaust, IN A FUCKING SMALL ENCLOSED ROOM UNTIL BRAIN DAMAGE OCCURRED!

Summer was equally as bad. We had to wear these flame retardant jumpsuits, which somehow managed to attract every solar ray from the sun imaginable! They were complete and total thermodynamic atrocities! Everyone hated them, and they were useless. If a major explosion ever occurred, WHAT THE HELL WERE THESE THINGS SUPPOSED TO DO ANYWAY?!? HELP IDENTIFY THE BODIES?!? So, I started going sans clothing under them. I tell this to the guys equally suffering there, and instead of being erotically excited, EVERYONE LOVED MY SUGGESTION! NOW EVERYONE IS NAKED AT WORK! "THIS WAS THE BEST IDEA, EVER!" they exclaimed with glee! Think outside of the box, people!

In times of stress induced mental collapse on my part, the younger guy upstairs that did the estimating, would be kind enough to sneak down to the lab room to help whenever he had time, because I honestly couldn't handle everything myself. No one would be able to, and I was supernaturally quick! Like a superhero of the concrete testing world! WHERE WAS MY CAPE?!? If you are unfamiliar with air meter testing devices, they look like a little like pressure cookers that you would use on your kitchen stove. And they are very, VERY expensive, about $600 or $700 worth. We are so busy, that one day, I thought he cleaned it out, and he thought I cleaned it out. You know what? NEITHER ONE OF US CLEANED IT OUT!!! So we come to work the next day to discover the unthinkable! The air meter was full of hardened concrete! I mean a completely adhered, dislodgeable mess! "OH, FUCK!!!" we both screamed in terror! And much like the efficiency that of a Damage Control Team, we devised a plan! I would use any implements available at this this shitty facility to chip this crap out! Meanwhile, he would sneak over to the garage and get a 5 gallon bucket of Gogo Goose, the chemical that the drivers used to clean the concrete off of their trucks (Known to cause prenatal cancer in California!). So an epic tale of chipping and swearing bonded us forever. Finally, after six hours, and much fudging of numbers to compensate for our incompetency, we had finally cleaned this pot, probably rivaling that of a cleaning frenzy of 1960's housewife on phenobarbital! Boy, did this thing sparkle when we were done!

This sealed our friendship forever! So we get sent off to a conference at Hiccups for cement. We drive separately, so when Jared parked on the train tracks, I managed to save his life (and his truck's life, as well)! We were sent down there in the winter time, and the train tracks CAME THROUGH THE PARKING LOT! If you worked there, you would obviously know this, but if it was your first rodeo there, death was probably imminent. There was absolutely NO fences, barriers, cones, ANYTHING! to let someone know NOT TO PARK THERE! This, combined with the fact that it had just snowed, rendered this death trap completely undetectable to the untrained eye! "JARED, MOVE YOUR TRUCK!" I shriek! "YOU ARE ON THE TRACKS!" He does and then comes out screaming, "WHAT?!? A TRAIN JUST COMES CRUISING THROUGH THIS PARKING LOT?!?" "YES! IT DOES!!!" (I only knew this, because I almost got hit by it one day driving my articulate truck there!) Boy, those things don't stop on a dime! (Both the trucks, or the trains, as well!)

Thankfully, by this point in time, we had managed to bond, because one morning before class, we were running late, so we run downstairs to grab a quick breakfast. I shove a WHOLE hard boiled egg in my mouth on the way out. (Once again, a terrible decision on my part. I seem to repeatedly have a problem in this department.) Suddenly, out in the parking lot, my gag reflexes unfortunately kicked in! (Apparently, I would never make a great porn star!) I stop walking, and start puking this egg everywhere! He turns around, and screams, "Jesus, God, are you OK?!?" White and yellow flying explosively everywhere, uncontrollably! I saved him from the train, but now it was his turn to save me from this killer ovum! By the time we got to class, both of us were laughing so hard, that we could barely pay attention!

If you have ever worked in the construction trade, everyone is a chain smoking alcoholic. Most people would denounce this practice, but with the long hours worked, it is probably the only way to maintain your sanity. So, one of the drivers there would always keep a cooler of beer on ice in the back of his truck. Everyone that wanted one had to leave a dollar in his cab. His truck, strewn with dollar bills, starts to resemble a seedy stripper joint. He starts screaming one day that this kind gesture is actually costing him money! It wasn't the booze, it was the ICE! Ok, don on my thinking helmet, Vaness! So, we had this cheap, shitty freezer in my poor excuse for a lab room (I'm not really actually sure even why it was in there in the first place. I didn't even have hot running water to wash out my lab equipment in the wintertime or heat, BUT I WAS EQUIPPED WITH THIS HIDEOUS ASTROCITY!) Anyways, so I started filling up the 6" X 12" plastic cylinders for testing with water and throwing them in there. Everyone knows that a bag of ice will melt quickly. The cubes are so small, that they will dissolve instantly in the heat, but these blocks would take forever to melt! Guess who got to drink for free! (On a side note, I'm not really sure of how great of an idea this was, because, on occasion this electrical abomination would short out, leaving my arm stuck to the open door, making it feel like a swarm of bees had managed to invade it! I would always manage to detach myself from this high voltage death appliance, but this always lead me to wonder what was killing more of my brain cells, this ancient icebox, or the alcohol!)

This episode brings me to the present owner. I was given a company truck, which transmission issues aside, I was very thankful for because I was allowed to take it home. Being the paranoid person that I am, I have an extra key made for it ($80 dollars out of my own pocket, thank you), because I was always afraid of getting locked out. So one Friday, we have our Christmas party in the garage. Everyone brought food and booze. I left without the company pickup, because I had been drinking, and didn't want to drive it home. I take it home on Sunday, whereas none to my knowledge, the owner sees me driving it on the way to church! On Monday, he shows up enraged. WHY THE HELL WAS I DOING DRIVING AROUND IN THE COMPANY PICKUP?!? (You'd swear that I was hauling something, like a load of lumber in the back!) I try and be respectful as possible, and tell him because I was drinking on Friday, I didn't want to drive it. Then, being the Sniveling Shit that he was, comes back with the worst retort that I have ever heard, "Well, I don't think you drank that much!" Logic, once again, where are you?!? Who says that reasonably to an employee? REALLY? WHAT? REALLY WHAT?!? I wait for Little Napoleon to finish his tirade, and calmly say, "Bob, I drank over half a box of red wine by myself, OK? I just didn't think driving was a God Damned good idea!" This rendered him speechless! Happy metabolisms out there to all of us physical laborers everywhere!

This fiasco leads me to the air conditioner episode. I hate the heat! I MEAN I REALLY FUCKING HATE IT! My Slovak heritage comes from colder climates, so I think that is the real issue. The lime baths combined with the fact that the windows didn't open, made the atmosphere in my office completely stifling in there. How much heat and humidity could one person be actually asked to endure?!? It was like being caught in a rain forest in Brazil in a vegetable steamer! Even the computer was sweating all over my desk! Everyone else upstairs had an air conditioner! Why couldn't I have one? So then one day I lose my temper and order one (once again, $300 out of pocket!) Because the windows wouldn't open to install it, I had to cut a hole in the wall by myself. I framed out the box, installed it, and even did trim work around it! Then The Sniveler bitches! I bought one that was too big for the room! WHAT?!? I'm not an electrician, but I managed to run a 10 gauge power line to the lime bath room to power this pig! Did he think there was some kind of invisible force field or vapor barrier, much rivaling something from Star Treck, that somehow managed to separate my nonexistent door to my office cubicle in the kitchen from the lime bath room or the front offices?!? He didn't even have to pay anyone to install it! I FUCKING DID! And wouldn't you rather a larger unit that would run less than a smaller one that would run all the time?!? What, you can run a concrete company, but not understand this concept?!? I'm sure those pricks are still using it to this day, and NOT COMPLAINING ABOUT IT!!! SURE, VANESS, DRIVE HOME SHITFACED IN THE COMPANY TRUCK, AND YOU SUCK FOR YOUR CARPENTRY EXPERTISE! GAME ON!

So now I am so pissed off, that I go out back to their defunct precast facility and swipe a couple of their forms. I start making 18 x 18 inch pavers with the leftover concrete from my tests, in ALL the plants. By the time I left there, I had about 1.300 square feet of them, which are now gracing my yard! Everywhere! Under sheds, a greenhouse, a walkway, you name it! The truck drivers and plant operators would actually help me! "I'M JUST HERE TO MAKE PAVERS ANYMORE!" I would indignantly yell! And I was, too!

Reason for Departure: A Sniveler Boss!

# Chapter 15

Bridge Inspection. Now PA has an enormous amount of funding for P3 and P4 bridge projects, so this basically means that these consultant companies will hire anyone with certifications and no bridge experience! They make their money like renting us out like Dollar A Night Whores! I was hired instantly. Inspect a bridge, they say! WHAT? What the hell do I know about bridges?!? FUCKING NOTHING! There was no training, anything! What was going on today in your reports? I don't know! There was a lot of stuff involving blacktop and concrete! Perhaps the creation of the universe! Ask God or Whoever, I was completely clueless! Ask my assistants Adam and Eve! While fashioning grape leaves to limit the imagination, they could probably give you X and Y coordinates of taking loose and core samples of bituminous material at every 500 tons. Also, the air meter results on QC, QA, AT, and VT air tests on concrete! Ask them where the cure box is and what the high and low temperatures are! Where are my incompetent assistants?!? Off trying to procreate the human race! Jesus Christ almighty! Where do you go to hire good help nowadays?!? These unemployment agencies suck!

<u>Reason for Departure:</u> I basically had ABSOLUTELY NO FUCKING CLUE WHAT I WAS DOING! You can only live the lie for so long. I once saw the movie from the 80's "Bright Lights, Big City," with Michael J. Fox. In it, he puts down that he could speak French on his resume. Well…he couldn't, AT ALL! So one day this lady calls him from Paris, and he completely vapor locks. Now everyone else in the office is staring at him sideways in his panic attack! That's how I felt! How's the densities today? WHAT? Parlez vous francais?!? Ou est la bibliotheque?

But I did give one hell of a parting gift! While in the midst of my employment there, I get sent for my NICET test. Now, this pissed me off, because initially I was sent for the wrong test that involved ASTM codes designed for government officials capable of accessing books worth $1,000 each! If you have ever tried to download these online, there is a big disclaimer, "Welcome, good morning AND GO FUCK YOURSELF!" I'm not shitting you! So, on the first try for the right one, I managed to pass the test for a Level II. "Well, you don't have enough work experience to be a Level II!" NICET indignantly proclaimed! "WELL, I PASSED YOUR FUCKING TEST, YOU BASTARDS! AND IT'S NOT BECAUSE I'M A GOOD GUESSER, EITHER!" What a fucking rip off! So now these cocksuckers want me to wait another year to resubmit my job experience, which I basically lied about at this point in time. Yes, I was working on SR this and that. Suddenly, I was approved for Level II. These fucking clowns. I could've said that I had experience in installing cell phone towers or decorating cakes for Christ Sakes! Fucking Jerkoff Scheme!

So this consultant company wanted their study folder back! I did! I sent it back to the Matamoras office! I get a statement from the bank, and realize that there is a "Stop Payment" on one of my checks! So, once again, phone calls were made in enragement! "Where is our folder?!?" they ask. "Where is my fucking paycheck?!?" I scream! "I am not driving to Allentown to deliver paperwork, when it's already in a company office! People visit from there all the time!" Think efficiency people!

<u>So this is the email I sent:</u> Hi Paula, I would like to discuss the matter of the coveted NICET folder. I have not responded, because I was somewhat upset by Deborah's e-mail. I did not steal this folder of double top secret documents. When I was originally hired at the Bored's Valley jobsite, I had mentioned that I was taking my NICET Materials test, and one of the inspectors were kind enough to suggest the folder that was in the storeroom and gave it to me to study from. Much like a literary whore, I honestly could not possibly say how many inspectors before myself have managed to fondle that used stack of bridge inspection material. It wasn't anyone's folder. It just lived on the storage room shelf like an old hooker on a deserted street corner. No one owned it. It was a master of its own destiny of accepting its own inspection johns. All I did was transport it from the Bored's Valley office to the one in Milford. But I have a dark secret, Paula! There's not one, but TWO NICET folders. YES…THAT'S RIGHT. I know it's shocking, but I would appreciate it if you kept this as our dirty, little secret, because I care about my fellow employees, and would not want Debbie to have an instant coronary. Now if I was a

thief or a vindictive person, I could have taken the second one and used it for kindling for my wood burner or perhaps produced some kind of hellacious paper mache project in the hopes of replicating Smaug, the Dragon from the Hobbit, (obviously not to scale, there's only probably about 150 pages there), and no one would be the wiser. I have not returned the folders yet because they are NOT MINE. And if you really consider the situation, if these books really are so important to McShit, how did TWO of them managed to get misplaced? I realize the importance of respecting McShit's property, but to state the obvious, all I would need to duplicate them would be to obtain a ream of paper, a $3.99 inch folder from Walmart, and an industrial Xerox machine, which working for McShit for the last year and a half, I've pretty much had access to on a daily basis.

I'd like to suggest to Debbie that perhaps a SWAT team should be organized for a reconnaissance mission. I know additional consultants of an obvious different profession may be needed, but I'm sure the state would see fit to allot additional funding in lieu of this terrible situation. There are some important facts that they should be aware of, though. The hostages are being kept against their will in the pantry. For their sake, at least I believe they are imprisoned in a serene environment, and as to my knowledge, have not been subjected to any unfathomable torture...yet. (Although I do believe that they are trapped between a bag of outdated Cool Ranch Doritos and a suspicious can of Dole crushed pineapple bits.) May I suggest having the crew enter in stealth mode on the North side of the building at perhaps between the hours of 1:00 AM to 3:00 AM, trying to take advantage of the narrow window of time between the day shift entering and the night shift leaving. Also, I'm sure that someone will be tempted to use the picnic table out back for aid in entrance, but it is pretty weather beaten, and no one deserves to be impaled on this mission. AND there is a strip of duct tape in the middle of the office floor holding the carpeting down. On occasion, it has known to loosen. No one needs to trip and suffer a concussion from the water cooler (that God Damned aqueous brute!) Just another prime example of, and as I have stated earlier, my extreme concern for the welfare of my fellow employees. Good luck, and God speed on this mission. Thank you!

Then the gentleman running the consulting company calls me completely insane! "Do you know that you could have been fired for that email?!?" Now, my favorite movie in life has always been "The Breakfast Club." I am not a very assertive person in nature, but when threatened with my back against the wall, I assume the rage disorder of one of those Komodo Dragons, probably trapped in a zoo, ill-fed, and with a low sugar tolerance disorder. Suddenly, I was channeling John Bender. "So what?" I say. Instantly, this man experienced utter confusion. I would like to parallel it to a gladiator trying to fight an invisible foe in an arena sans weapon, and without the added spectators. And he says, "WHAT?I?" And in this sudden confrontational disaster, it rendered his mind in complete disarray. And much like channeling Andrew Clark in that movie, I say, "Did I stutter?" "WHAT?!?" He says again. Was this a Beatles album? How many more times did I have to hear the words, "No. 9," again?!?" So this man basically throws his tail between his legs and begs me to please behave to the best of my ability. Well, there were some dead wishes right there!

Everyone starts getting into the act of my sarcasm! One day, sick of dealing with mindless governmental reign, I suggest that maybe DOT should do a study on the effects of roadkill or urine on our blacktop. And here was the other idea I presented on how to fill potholes. What if everyone who drove on the roads just were forced to chew a pack a gum a day while driving, and had to aim for these treacherous asphalt caverns! DOT was already wasting enough of our tax payer dollars, in my opinion! Why not just shoot for the Moon?!?

So the DOT official in charge writes a fake Job Posting: <u>Foliage Urine Carcass Regional Specialist.</u> Description of Duties: This new position, Foliage Urine Carcass Regional Specialist or FUCRS, is responsible for developing, analyzing, and implanting the study, effects and treatments for the potential deterioration, safety and remedy for the related to Foliage Urine and Carcass repercussions to the roadways throughout the Commonwealth. Duties will include the development of "Teams" to study, analyze, and develop treatments and materials to combat this matter of contention. There will be four areas of concern which the Teams will be built around. They are as follows:

<u>First:</u> With the Commonwealth's vast use of Superpave Wearing Courses, a Team would need to be developed to concentrate on the repercussions of these compounds on this type of Wearing Surface. The Team will be defined as SUPER.

<u>Second:</u> Analysis of these compounds, Foliage, Urine, and Carcasses, will need to be compiled and studied to determine the effects of these elements on our wearing Surfaces. Including Superpave, Nova Chip, Oil and Chip, etc…The Team will be defined as ANAL.

<u>Third:</u> Another Team will be needed to determine the Skid-resistance, Treatment and Utilization Procedures needed to combat the effects these compounds have on the slickness of the Wearing Surface prior to their deterioration. Also, the need to develop a Skid-resistance Treatment and develop Procedures on how to utilize this. The Team will be defined as Skid Treatment and Utilization Procedure Development or STUPD.

<u>Fourth:</u> The final Team will need to determine the Materials needed to be utilized and applied to prevent the slickness effects these compounds have on the Wearing Surface. Materials that may need to be utilized in the interim until all the other Teams' findings are complete and developed. When final analysis is complete, additional materials may need to be Analyzed and Developed to determine effectiveness to combat this problem. The Team will be defined as Material Unit Development Analyst or MUDA.

With the Teams in place, SUPER ANAL STUPD MUDA FUCRS, The Department hopes to provide a new direction to an age old problem.

This is the mentality of DOT. People actually started applying for this job! Oh, my God, someone just kill me already!

<u>Reason for Departure:</u> I just blatantly hated doing this for a living. And everyone was stupid, except for the guy who wrote this soliloquy.

<u>Pour It, Slam It Precast.</u> Oh, God. Have you ever shown up to a job interview, and instead of being riddled with anxiety, you are like, "Holy, hell! What I am doing here? This place is absolutely retarded! There is probably nothing I can either do or say to screw this up!" Upon initial arrival, I noted that the grounds to this place looked like some dystopian future, riddled with machinery that would rival "Mad Max Beyond Thunderdome". Warehouses were scattered throughout a nonstop swirling dusty wasteland, and androids roamed everywhere! OHSA where are you?!? Now, the girl who was training me was INCREDIBLY knowledgeable, but also INCREDIBLY pregnant! I have not had children myself, but I DO have sympathy for women in the "Family Way."

In spite of the environmental conditions, and her own as well, she was unbelievably patient with me. Not only did I have to learn how to read Plans and Specs, but this company would manufacture its products in a myriad of ways – sideways, upside down, somehow in a different dimension by David Copperfield, etc. So, not only did one have to be able to read these engineer's drawings, one would also have to be able to flip them around in their mind while being manufactured. This required quite the intellectual feat almost that of Stephen Hawking! Let's try and build a box culvert today off of these stoner's plans! Hey, it's only going to support a bridge! Fuck bridges already! These engineers were so loopy, that they would design drainage units with 26" holes ON

THE SAME SIDE AS THE STAIRS! HOW THE FUCK WAS ANYONE SUPPOSED TO GET UP OR DOWN WITH LIMITED UPPER ARM STRENGTH?!? PUT THE STAIRS ON THE OPPOSITE BLANK SIDE, YOU JACKASSES! JESUS CHRIST, IT DOESN'T TAKE A FUCKING ROCKET SCIENTIST TO FIGURE THIS OUT!!! How the hell was I expected to inspect this crap?

There were literally thousands of units that would get shipped into the yards every day. Vaness, check this unit and that. Much like my face blindness disorder, WHERE THE HELL DID EVERTHING GO? No lots were labeled, and everything looked the same to me! It was like trying to navigate a vast sea of mismatched concrete monoliths! Help me Magellan! I'm on foot in the area the size of, and much resembling, the Gobi desert hoping to locate these pieces before they would be carelessly thrown on trailers and shipped out. By the time they would be unloaded from the warehouses, taken by the loaders to the storage areas, and then reloaded, they would unfortunately resemble the amount of damage inflicted on some poor prostitute that had failed to give their pimp his proper cut! Shit would be smashed, broken, basically destroyed, etc! Then letters of apology would have to be written to the state. "Sorry this unit was delivered in such poor condition! Hopefully it will still be salvageable on your jobsite! I assure you that our facilities really do have the capabilities of manufacturing a high quality product (on occasion). Have a nice day! Regards, V." OH MY GOD! Now, I was qualified to run the lab room, so on top of fruitlessly trying to chase this junk around, I would have to cover for this technician when he needed time off. Break these cylinders! Keep the paperwork up to date! Do these gradations and wash tests! Climb up a three story ladder to get moisture probe samples! WHAT THE FUCK WAS ON THAT TRAILER THAT JUST LEFT?!?

The only redeeming value of this company, was that it was like working in an asylum. Everyone employed there was completely crazy, but no matter how busy they were, they always made time to help each other out. This was coupled by the fact that these 4000 pound pieces were being lifted over your head, so you would basically spend the day praying that one of the chains wouldn't snap, whereas you would be crushed like a bug with a weak exoskeleton smacked off a car windshield driving about a hundred miles an hour! BUT! The warehouses had EXCELLENT speaker systems, where we would be allowed to listen to the Insane Clown Posse everyday. If you are unfamiliar with this group, all of their songs are about as belligerent as I am, but they all had an unholy beat, much to rival that of ZZ Tops' Velcro Fly. This was indeed fortunate, because I believe the thumping bass managed to drown out most of our terrified prayers!

<u>Reason for Departure:</u> Fuck this dump already!

# Chapter 16

<u>Back to bridge inspection.</u> I worked with this outfit called Kreeper, and much like my experience with Rigatoni Excavators, there was a complete sense of lawlessness there. I got stuck working on a job 112 miles from my house, which basically took me three hours each way depending on traffic. The only redeeming value was, these workers were certifiably nuts, also! We start working on this bridge in the fall when the leaves were down and crunchy. Well, not only trolls live under bridges, BUT ALSO GIGANTIC MOTHER FUCKING RIVER SPIDERS!!! SOMEONE NEEDS TO DO A STUDY ON THESE! They were so big, that I would be sitting down on an embankment doing my paperwork and hear rustling approaching. OH, NO, IT'S ONE COMING IN FOR A VICTIM…ME! MY WORST FEAR WITH EIGHT LEGS COMING RIGHT AT ME! FUCKING CHRIST HELP ME! I mean, how big does something have to be to make noise in the woods? A 250 pound bear, a 120 pound deer? No, A HUGE, CREEPING, HUNGRY SPIDER!

One day the guys were hauling sandbags in the water and somehow one of these demons the size of my palm ends up on his arm! It's like it just materialized out of nowhere! (What kind of hellacious properties of terror and teleportation did these things possess?!?) The amount of screaming and shouting that occurred were epic! Finally, this hell spawn ended up in the river! The guy who was tortured, got even, though, to the main heckler. He kills a baby Copperhead snake one day and sneaks up to this guy, AND HITS HIM WITH IT IN HIS FACE! More epic shrieking occurred! I felt like I was running some kind of shady day care center! Children crying, "He threw a spider on me! Well, he hit me in the face with a snake!" What's a mother to do?!? YOU ASSHOLES!

Have you ever had a premonition about total disaster occurring? Well, we were supposed to clean out the sediment of the underside of the bridge on a Friday. They send down an operator with a Skid Steere to do it. If you are unfamiliar with these machines, they are about the size and shape of R2D2 from Star Wars. This kid starts digging, and mud starts engulfing his machine! Now it is trapped, like a dinosaur in the La Brea Tar Pits! This disaster was only exponentially magnified by my boss from DOT showing up. Damage Control, where are you?!? Of all times, REALLY?!? We had a ton of lumber cut down from around the jobsite. Me living in the country, and am used to getting stuck 4 wheeling in the mud, I SUGGEST perhaps rolling some of the said timber under the tracks for traction. If you lined them up parallel, and had the machine put its bucket down, you could push them under using the excavator that was there already. My boss goes crazy! "Don't suggest anything to the contractor!" he screams at me and then leaves! After an hour and a half of extreme deliberation, a plan was devised! "Let's put logs underneath this machine!" GREAT IDEA ORIGINAL THOUGHT PERSON!

The one thing DEP is very strict about, is having machinery in a river. So when there was no way to remove this mired thing, I say to the manager, "Listen, I'm going for a twenty minute walk over to the shitter. Wherever this thing ends up, I guess I missed everything!" They end up dragging this submerged mechanical beast across, which, by time I returned, was completely accomplished. Ok, back on to inspection. Suddenly, BOOM! Apparently, the kid that was driving it, cruised through the woods on the far side, AND MANAGED TO FLIP IT OVER IN A DRAINAGE DITCH! This unforeseeable act was probably not his fault. These are absolutely terrible to see out of! Everyone is scrambling! An excavator had to be tracked off the site over to the travesty! The kid was OK, but it took a hell of amount of skill to try and upright this machine! They were only able to push it out of the ditch, not pull it out! So now this thing is still trapped in the forest on the wrong side of the river! "My boss was going to kill me!" I start screaming!

"Don't worry!" I was assured! "We're leaving for the weekend, but we'll fix this situation!" RIGHT, AND THE CHECK IS IN THE MAIL, AND I LOVE YOU! Well, I get there early on Monday, and the machine is missing! Did fairies show up over the weekend and take it to some magical realm?!? Was some zeppelin hired to air lift this yellow device out of the woods? WHAT?!? Well, these fabulous guys came in before their shift started and not get paid and made a make shift road on the far bank, whereas they towed this thing back across the river and up the embankment, just to save my ass from getting caned! What gentlemen!

However, said gentlemen screwed me on one occasion. Now, being a woman in this profession, this is terrible. When you are riding "The Cotton Pony," and facilities are nil to begin with, things have a tendency to make you a bit crabby. That's OK, I'll just clean up in the river! One day after visiting the shitter in the dark, before anyone else got there, I realized the unthinkable had happened! There was NO GOD DAMNED TOILET PAPER! I HAD TO USE THE CARDBOARD ROLL!!! God, Grant Me Strength to Endure This Hardship! I texted the manager, and told him that I was shutting this job down until two ply was delivered! Well, much like rubbing a genie in a bottle, my wishes were granted! Now I got back at these guys for my feminine hygiene suffering. Being stuck under the bridge and very far away from the green office, it was just easier for them to open the double doors on their trucks and take a leak there. Also, by this point in time, everyone felt so comfortable around me that everyone just started doing it next to me! So I got my revenge! I would sneak up behind them, and, much like the river spiders searching for helpless prey, in the midst of their golden cascade, I WOULD PUSH THEM AS HARD AS I COULD! "GOD DAMN IT VANESS, I JUST PISSED ON MY LEG, IN MY TRUCK, ON MY TOOLS, etc." would be randomly shrieked much to my delight! Don't ever let a roll go empty again, you ASSHOLES! No more screaming was administered until…

The next time I got screamed at by my boss. He shows up, and I am trying to help the female technician there make 18, 6 X 12 inch cylinders. I actually have more certifications than him (seriously, DOT requires the least amount). Having suffered in this industry, I have complete sympathy for anyone struggling to do what I used to do! "Stop helping her. We could get sued!" this fat, lazy fuck shrieks! So now the concrete truck gets jammed up. The poor kid that was driving it was almost in tears! I go bouncing up the ladders on the front of it to help him shovel the rest of the load off. Never in my life, have I seen the look of such gratitude! Once again, I get screamed at by my boss! "We're not here to help, just to observe!" I'm sorry, but I'm not going to sit by, and watch someone struggle, "YOU FUCKING FAT, LAZY PANTYWASTE! I'm still getting my paperwork done on time! What the hell is your problem?!?" I mentally scream!

I don't want to be morose, but I remember watching clips of the Milgram Experiments of 1963 whereas most people, when instructed by an authoritative figure, will obey them, hurting any subjects rendered powerless in their control. Well, not me, baby! I don't care what is going on, I'M NOT LETTING ANYONE SUFFER! KEEP SCREAMING AT ME! I DON'T CARE! I WAS NOT RAISED TO BE A COLD HEARTED BASTARD! I might curse a lot and not go to church, but I believe I am a good person. I will always give a hitchhiker a ride, and give someone in need a place to stay! And I am sure as shit, not going to sit by on a jobsite, and WATCH SOMEONE HELPLESSLY FLAIL ABOUT LIKE A FISH OUT OF WATER!

Another time my DOT boss proved himself to be an asshole, was when he requested that I drive three hours EACH WAY to the jobsite ON CHRISTMAS EVE! "I need you to watch that technician strip those cylinders and put them back into the cure box." he says. Now, if you are unfamiliar with the concrete industry, it's poured into these 6" X 12" cylinders on a site, which go into a box that's either heated or cooled, depending on the weather. Then the plastic is stripped off of them, and they are taken to a place to get crushed in a giant contraption called a "Break Machine" to test for compaction strength. Now, this is what pissed me off! The plant that gave us the concrete wasn't even open, so I couldn't break them even if I wanted to!!! So this little adventure was completely illogical! "Sir, it's Christmas Eve, do you even know how much more traffic will be on the roads?!?" I politely ask. "JUST DO IT, VANESSA!!!" he screams! (Ya, and I bet that JERKOFF wouldn't be working!!!) So I agreed, but then I called the tech (who I didn't even know at the time) that was working, and explain my tale of woe, and he says the coolest thing ever, "Vaness, I don't even know what you are talking about, because you've been here ALL DAY supervising me!" How could some people be such INCONSIDERATE FUCKS, and others be so FUCKING WONDERFUL?!? That was the BEST Christmas gift ever!!!

Another day, this douche boss of mine from DOT calls me and demands numbers and drawings from underneath the bridge beams. So I get out my graph paper and start drafting. It takes me three hours in freezing water, but I believe I ended up with results to rival any engineer with his ass parked in any comfortable office any day. Sketches and 50 some calculations done without a computer or a job trailer. This dork shows up, and then proceeds to tell me that, "This isn't an art class, Vanessa! All you had to do was draw me some arrows!" The manager waits until he leaves, and then asks me seriously, "Are you OK? Because I know how long and how much you suffered to do that. Really, I honestly feel bad, and your boss just basically cruelly ruined your good intentions! And I'll tell you why. He probably couldn't have done that himself, and just felt nervous, because he is inferior to your abilities." Said Asshole didn't have the problem of using all my drafting for his office books, though! That was the last straw! I just stopped basically giving a shit anymore, so I started blatantly screwing off!

Welcome to The Dr. Suess Jobsite:

Draw me a bridge! Draw me a ridge! Draw me some arrows. Maybe some sparrows? How about some God Damn wheelbarrows?!?

So now I start drawing pictures of anything. Maybe it was a dragon under the bridge lighting our equipment on fire, or me as a mermaid being dragged around by an excavator, I just really didn't really give a fuck! (Needless to say, NONE OF THOSE PICTURES EVER ENDED UP IN MY BOSS'S BOOK!)

I now have a 5 Dollar bet with the manager that is running this operation, which I managed to lose. The one thing I value in life, is honesty, so I paid up being a total dick. I counted out exactly 5 dollars worth of change in my truck, and then proceeded to open his truck door AND THROW

IT EVERYWHERE IN THERE! "GOD DAMN IT, VANESS! IT'S BEEN TWO WEEKS, AND I AM STILL PICKING OUT QUARTERS!" Was proclaimed, along with a lot of company door locking from that point on! I managed to find his keys in the back of his pickup one day, and left a note tied around them, "Try harder next time!" it read!

One day, I wanted my rebar numbers. And was repeatedly declined by time after time by the manager. So, I go crazy, and after work when I asked again and was told no, I blow a fuse! This guy is sitting in his Ford 150 with the concrete foreman in the passenger seat. The truck is running, which is very loud, so he never heard the disaster until it was too late. I launch myself on the hood, and manage to wriggle up to the windshield. Now comedic violence ensues! The manager looks up from his paperwork and screams, "Get off my hood you crazy Bitch!" "I want my numbers, you Prick!" I yell back! Everyone knows from the movies, that the easiest way to get someone (or something) off of the front of your vehicle, is to go as fast as you can AND THEN SLAM ON YOUR BRAKES! That's what happened! He takes off down the road with me on the hood and then does it! Well, being well versed in cinematography, I know enough to lock my fingers under the hood! The concrete foreman is repeatedly shrieking, "OH MY GOD, WE ARE ALL GOING TO BE FUCKING FIRED AROUND HERE!" Not when someone has a 4,000 PSI death grip on your hood! The manager finally returns to the parking area, and we both watch the concrete foreman hyperventilate! "Fine, here's your numbers!" the manager screams! Really, why did that have to be so painful?!?

The complete belligerence didn't end there, though. One day, I was going over numbers with the manager there, when a lady blows through a flagger's stop sign. This man screeches, "STOP!!!" Then, after twenty yards later, she miraculously does, BUT THEN WHIPS HIM THE FINGER!!! Then he drops his sign, and starts trying to rip her out of car, all while bellowing, "I'LL KICK YOU IN YOUR BOX, YOU DUMB FUCKING CUNT!" Several things simultaneously managed to occur at this point. I fell down at the side of the manager's truck, and was laughing so hard, that I was trying not to orgasmacally pee myself! And then the manager goes racing off to tackle this guy! What kind of a jobsite was this?!? What more weirdness could be possibly tolerated?!?

On the final day of completion, the contractor was leveling out a grassy parking area around where they used to leave their equipment. I have no attention span, and so I start wandering about, like a child that should be on Ritalin. Suddenly, I find, what to my standards, should be equal to the Ark of the Covenant (I set my bar REALLY low). There is this toy baby doll lying there where we are working, somehow cast aside. Where did this thing come from? What child had misplaced it? How did it manage to not get squashed under the equipment? (So many unanswered questions, much like my job history!) It was filthy, and I don't know if you remember these, but old dolls used to have eyes that would open and close depending on what angle you held them. This creepy ability and the fact that it was basically just gross, was absolutely just terrifying! What necromancer could possibly resuscitate this discarded angel? So I did the only thing I thought possible! I put it in the manager's driver's seat, strapped in, with a note stuck on it that said, "Daddy, where have you been?!?" Instead of screaming, the manager picks it out gingerly, and proclaims, "Boy, is thing going to have a hard time in life!" And then proceeds to unceremoniously toss it into the back of his pickup. Hopefully, better horizons will be had for that once loved CREEPY ASS THING! CREEPY ASS THING, please send me a postcard in regards to your general well being! Then the unthinkable occurred to me. My family is VERY superstitious, which has managed to instill terrible values upon me! What if I had awoken CREEPY ASS from its eternal slumber only to piss it off?!? Now I am sleeping with one eye open, a 9 MM, and Potato Rock. Potato, if I should happen to doze, keep an eye out for me! (Caution, terrible, corny joke inserted here!) Well, Potato was apparently very diligent in his spud like capabilities, because I am still alive!

Now we are throwing hay bales from the 7000 ton dump truck to completely finish the job. The manager (being as helpful as usual) is tossing them off. The only problem was, the kid driving it couldn't drive a stick shift, (even I could drive one, but hey, everyone's gotta learn somewhere. Double entendre, anyone?), so everytime the kid would stall, the manager would flip over into the hay. "God Damn it! You are 35 years old, and you still can't drive a standard?!?" he would scream! Kabam! Over he would go again! "You're lucky I'm not stoned like I usually am, or I'D BE DOING A MUCH WORSE JOB!" the kid retorted! Good point!

The last day on this jobsite finally rage disorder descends upon me! A bunch of engineering kids were hired go and check this jobsite out! Did they have to spend most of the winter freezing their asses off like I did, getting paid half as much as the laborers? No! They sat in their warm offices after mommy and daddy finished paying their college bills! They show up in 50 degree weather with their Alaskan Survival Gear donned on, complete with knitted mittens and hats from grandma, and proclaim, "I think we will need an extra rock over here!" "Thank you, for letting me know, I will get right on that!" I say. Was I actually seeing this spectacle or was it a mirage of some kind torturous mental insanity?!! I was so pissed off, that I just left right in the middle of the day!

<u>Reason for Departure:</u> Fired for too much leniency with the contractor and basically unruly fuckery on my part. Good!

This is basically why I wrote this book. Someone, somewhere has to know my pain of unappreciation and loathing for DOT and the vast majority of major management everywhere! To channel the Rolling Stones, doesn't anyone have any sympathy for the devil? You decide!

Hopefully my career in this path has come to an end. There is only so much weirdness and depravity one can deal with! Come on Potato, we are on to new and different disasters awaiting us!

FIN!

Printed in the United States
By Bookmasters